A Thunder Bird in Bomber Command

To Jean

Win my very best wishes!

THUNDER
BIRD
in Bomber Command

The Wartime Letters and
Story of Lionel Anderson,
the Man Who Inspired
a Legend.

Sean Feast
Foreword by Shane Rimmer

Published in 2015 by Fighting High Ltd,
www.fightinghigh.com

British Library Cataloguing-in-Publication data.
A CIP record for this title is available from the
British Library.

ISBN – 13: 978-0992620776

Designed and typeset in Adobe Minion 11/15pt
by Michael Lindley, www.truthstudio.co.uk.

Printed and bound in China by Toppan Leefung.
Front cover design by www.truthstudio.co.uk.

To my brothers, Gary and Stuart, and for the happy memories that Gerry Anderson's creations gave us as children.

Contents

Foreword *by Shane Rimmer*

Shane Rimmer is a legend in the world of Gerry Anderson productions, providing one of the most recognisable voices in Supermarionation history for Thunderbirds' *Scott Tracy. He has featured in over fifty films in the UK and Europe, and appeared in numerous TV roles, including* Space 1999 *and* UFO.

What remained an intriguing mystery for many of Gerry Anderson's audiences on his continued run of TV successes was 'How does he come up with so many gripping story ideas and the ever exciting gadgetry that goes with them?' One after another they just seemed to tumble out on to UK television screens for both young and old alike – *Supercar*, *Fireball XL5*, *Stingray*, *Thunderbirds*, *Captain Scarlet*, *Joe 90*, *UFO*, *Space 1999*, *The Protectors* and *Dick Spanner*. It was an awesome output. And it didn't stop there.

Following the incredible success *Thunderbirds*, almost in the blink of an eye his productions were beginning to show on TV networks around the world, from Japan to the Middle East, to America, Scandinavia and Europe. It was unstoppable. All kinds of speculation and theories were offered as to what fuelled Gerry's mighty determination. They were all wide of the mark. But Gerry knew.

The inspiration was direct and personal – from his elder brother Lionel who had given up his life as a pilot during the Second World War. Gerry never forgot where that inspiration had sprung from. He was much too young to follow in his brother's footsteps, but there were other ways in which he would show his most profound regard for all that his brother had given. Every move and thought in his spectacular rise up the show business ladder had been influenced by that regard.

Recently recovered documents, in the form of Lionel's letters home, that contain observations, thoughts and reminiscences during his wide ranging and incident-filled travels, form the basis of this fascinating story.

There is much more to the book than the letters. There is the story of Lionel's war, a secret war, and the part he played in it. It is a terrific story, full of great detail and research that shows how Lionel's love for flying and manner of death had such a powerful and profound influence on Gerry and his career.

The author has told a striking and authentically true tale of two brothers, each making their own way in different countries, thousands of miles apart, yet maintaining that mystic bond that maybe only brothers have the privilege of sharing.

Shane Rimmer
December 2014

Lionel in a formal portrait, having recently been awarded his wings and his sergeant's stripes.

Prologue

It had been a fine day with a fresh wind. Conditions overnight were due to improve slightly and there was little by the way of cloud. A clear enough sky to see the target; sufficient cloud in which to hide if trouble stirred. The perfect hunting weather, only tonight they were not hunting rabbits or foxes but more cunning beasts: German night fighters.

Intruders they were called. Very fast, low-flying Mosquitoes – twin-engined marvels made in furniture factories and dubbed 'wooden wonders' after their plywood and glue construction. Powered by two Rolls-Royce Merlin engines, the 'Mossie' could reach speeds well in excess of 350mph and fly to Berlin and back if necessary.

In the nose of the aircraft was its 'sting' – four 20mm cannon and four .303 machine guns, capable of tearing through the thin metal fabric of an enemy aircraft or the frail bodies of its crew and doing terrible damage. Capable, also, of taking out gun emplacements, flak positions and other 'targets of opportunity'. And the Mosquito could carry bombs too. In this case two 250lb bombs in its belly and two more bombs under the wings. What it couldn't shoot it could blast to pieces with high explosives or rockets, or burn with incendiaries. It was not fussy. The Mosquito FBVI was a fighter-bomber, and appropriately named.

The crew had been briefed earlier in the day. It was, in fact, their first night intruder operation since their squadron had re-equipped with the Mosquito only a few weeks earlier. Not that the pilot was inexperienced. He was a flight sergeant and had already survived more than twelve months of operations, stooging up and down the French coast in an obsolete Boulton Paul Defiant equipped with a mysterious magical set to confound the enemy defenders and a rear gunner to ward off unwanted attention. It had been painstaking and even occasionally boring work, yet an essential part of the wider bombing war, the Second Front in the air.

He had exchanged Defiants for the Mosquito, like swapping a donkey for a thoroughbred racehorse, and was enjoying the thrill of low flying at high speed. Now they were detailed to patrol the area around the airfield at Venlo, one of no fewer than thirteen aircraft that would be buzzing around Venlo, Bonn, Twente, St Trond, Gilze-Rijen and Evere, waiting to catch a glimpse of a light on the ground or a blink in the air that could betray a German night fighter. Then they would slip in behind, thumb the buttons that would fire the guns and all hell would break loose. If they were lucky. If they were not seen by the ground defences. But they had the darkness to protect them. And their speed. And surprise, although the element of surprise was beginning to wear thin. The Germans now expected these attacks, had come to fear them. They even had a word for it: *MoskitoPanik*.

The pilot of Mosquito NS895 taxied his aircraft to the end of the runway and the point of take-off, his navigator perched on his right-hand side and slightly below, waiting to play his role, guiding men and machine over the channel and across the enemy coast to the target. The pilot waited for the 'Green' from control. He trimmed the elevator to make the aircraft slightly nose heavy, eased the rudder a fraction to the right and kept the ailerons neutral. The fuel cocks were fully on, ready for the off. Props to maximum revs, the engine noise gradually increasing with the surge in power. Flaps up. Radiators open. Brakes off. Rolling forward. Picking up speed now and opening the throttles slowly. Adjusting the tail wheel, keeping the aircraft straight and true, watching the tendency to swing. Plus 9 boost. Much faster now, 150 knots and leaving mother earth. Wheels up. Trim the aircraft now to tail heavy and climbing at plus 7 with 2,650 revs and easing her into the inky blackness of the night. It is just before 1.00am.

The first of the night intruders begin landing back at base four hours later, apart from an 'early return' or two experiencing trouble with their navigation equipment. It is to be expected. Their technology is good, revolutionary even, but prone to failure. There is a buzz of excitement at interrogation and in the crew room. The wingco has had a productive night, dropping fragmentation bombs and incendiaries on Quakenbrück, hoping to have inflicted some damage. He had seen the runway, briefly, before the lights had been doused. One of the flight commanders has had similar fun, but is not sure of the results.

Luckiest of the night, however, is the squadron's resident 'star', its very own Dambuster 'Micky' Martin. Not content with blowing up dams over

Germany, Martin is now having a go as an intruder, and a highly successful one. Tonight he has attacked an enemy aircraft, a Junkers 88 he thinks, and damaged it. He has attacked another aircraft on the ground, giving it a two-second burst and seeing a flash that might have been a fire, and this one he believes he has destroyed.

One aircraft, however, is overdue. By now it will have run out of fuel so can no longer be in the air. It might have landed at another airfield, it happens often, but as yet there is no news. Nothing has been heard from the aircraft or the crew since they took off. Repeated attempts at reaching them on the radio go unanswered. The inevitable has to be acknowledged. The crew is posted as 'missing'.

Now the administrative system moves into full swing. A telegram is dictated to be sent to the next of kin. They all begin in the same way. 'Regret to inform you that your son … is missing as a result of air operations. …' The adjutant drafts a letter, to be signed by the officer commanding as if he has written it himself: 'I held your son in the highest esteem, more especially as I have heard of the sterling work he has performed since he joined the squadron. He was popular with his comrades. …'

Hours later the telegram will be received by a fearful family at a house in north London. Trembling hands will read but fail to comprehend or accept the words printed on the flimsy beige paper. Their son: missing. Missing.

Their son who had been his mother's most precious gift. Their son who had always loved flying and a sense of adventure. Their son who had spent almost two years training in the US, and who had met film stars and even appeared in a movie – the *Thunder Birds*. Their son who often teased his younger brother Gerry, a little boy who idolised his older sibling nonetheless, and would never truly come to terms with his loss and the pain it would cause. Missing. Dead.

Flight Sergeant Lionel Anderson had taken his final flight.

Lionel in his uniform as a stretcher bearer in the early days of the war.

Chapter 1

Volunteer

Lionel Anderson had always wanted to fly. As a little boy he had grown up making model aircraft and feasting on stories of the First World War heroes and their flying adventures. If ever war came, he promised himself, he would be as great a fighter ace as Mannock or McCudden, and more famous than Ball. At least he could dream.

He was born in 1922 in Westcliff-on-Sea, a rather bleak seaside town overlooking the Thames Estuary. His family had lived there for almost three decades; his grandfather, who had arrived in the UK from a tiny Russian village in the province of Grodno (now in Poland), was an established and well-respected member of the Ceylon Road Synagogue that he had helped to establish.

His parents, Joseph (Joe) and Deborah (Debbie), however, did not live in Westcliff long before breaking camp and moving to north London, firstly to Willesden and then soon after to west Hampstead before finally putting down roots at an address in Neasden Lane at the heart of the local Jewish community.

The grandfather had changed his Russian name, Bielogovski, to 'Abrahams', so the story went, on the suggestion of the immigration officer when he had arrived in the country some fifty years earlier. The family name remained Abrahams until at least 1940, after which it changed again to Anderson on the prompting of Lionel's mother, understood to be a deliberate attempt to distance the name from its Jewish origins and the prejudice that went with it at that time.

By all accounts Lionel enjoyed a happy childhood but it was not without its difficulties. Money was often in short supply, and their house in west Hampstead was little more than a bedsit, Lionel sharing a single room with his parents and younger brother, Gerald. His father had worked in the family clothing business, but had argued with his brother and left, taking a job installing and maintaining tobacco dispensing machines. It was hard work that paid little, and their lack of wealth and prosperity caused friction in the house. Arguments were the norm, and Joe would clash with his wife (it was not a love match) and their friends over money and his ardently held socialist views. Even when he supplemented his income by providing private tuition to young boys and girls wishing to learn the piano (he was a classical pianist), there was seldom enough in the house to get by.

Lionel was educated first at the Mora Road School in Cricklewood, an imposing red-brick primary school on the edge of Dollis Hill, and then after at the Kingsgate Road School before concluding his schooling at Fleet Central, Gospel Oak. (The school was used as a fire station later in the war and was completely destroyed by a flying bomb in 1944.) He was also an active member of the scouting fraternity, an activity that no doubt helped to further heighten his sense of adventure. All hopes of pursuing any kind of peacetime career of his own choice ended in September 1939 with the outbreak of war when he volunteered, at the age of seventeen and a half, as a part-time stretcher-bearer in the Gibbons Division of Willesden Civil Defence Service.

By the autumn and winter of 1940, with the Battle of Britain lost to the Germans, their air force – the still mighty Luftwaffe – had turned its attention to bombing London in a period of the war known as the Blitz. Thousands of tons of high explosives and incendiaries were dropped on the capital causing massive destruction, killing and maiming thousands of civilian men, women and children. If the Germans thought that they could bomb the British people into submission, they were to be sorely disappointed, however, and the bombing, if anything, did more to stiffen the resolve of Londoners everywhere.

Although the principal targets were the docks, warehouses and manufacturing installations in the East End, almost every part of the City and Greater London experienced some damage, either intentionally or by accident, and the Willesden Civil Defence Service was kept busy. It had been set up before the war for just such an eventuality, and now it was putting its training into practice, co-ordinating its activities across a broad range of disciplines from air-raid wardens to ambulance drivers – what today might be termed 'first responders'. It was certainly not without its risks. On 11 September 1940, Frank Vaughan, an air-raid precaution (ARP) warden with the Willesden force, was killed in a bombing raid as a result of injuries received through flying shrapnel.

Lionel had some exciting experiences of his own to tell his friends about, but also had to stare death in the face and deal with the seriously injured. No doubt this involvement made him more determined to knock the German aggressors from the skies. It also convinced his parents that his younger brother, Gerald, should be evacuated – sent to live a safe distance away in the country with foster parents. He hated it.

Joining the Royal Air Force could seem a daunting prospect for a young aspiring eagle. Determined to fly, Lionel headed down to his nearest Recruitment Centre to fill out the necessary forms and put his name forward as a volunteer for aircrew. Then he waited until summoned to an Aircrew Selection Board where he was interviewed and asked a series of personal questions about his education, interests and physical well-being. Then came the intelligence tests – with a particular focus on mathematics – after which he was subjected to a rigorous medical examination. Having been deemed to be of the right calibre – with sufficient academic prowess and background (snobbery was rife in 1940s Britain) – Lionel was passed fit for pilot training, sent home, and asked to be patient. A few weeks later a letter arrived asking for him to report to the Aircrew Reception Centre (ACRC) at Regent's Park.

Nearly every young man who joined the RAF wanted to fly, but only a small percentage ever made it. Indeed, at one point it was reckoned that as few as 13% of those who turned up at the ACRC even got to see the insides of an aircraft.

Some were rejected for pilot training from the outset and, if of suitable intelligence, were steered towards becoming an observer – a category of aircrew later split into two: navigator and air bomber. Others were encouraged instead to volunteer for one of the 'trades' – a wireless operator, air gunner or flight engineer (at least later in the war). The advantage of becoming an air gunner, for example, was that it required a far shorter period of training, meaning that the most eager of the recruits could be in the fighting war within six months. Pilot training, however, could take upwards of two years, and there was no guarantee of passing the course. Many a navigator or bomb aimer, if not initially destined for the role, had started life wanting to be a pilot, but had failed to make the grade and been 'remustered' – Service parlance for being 'washed out' and given a different job.

At ACRC Lionel spent nearly three weeks living in a once very elegant corner of Regent's Park, one contemporary describing aircrew cadets as 'living like weevils in a long line of luxury flats overlooking the canal, with windows bricked up and bells outside to warn of gas attacks'. At the beginning, the men were all in civilian dress, and paraded around the streets of St John's Wood. Only later were they issued with their stiff, new uniforms, and allowed to wear a distinctive white 'flash' in the cap band to denote an airmen who had volunteered for aircrew training.

All of the men, Lionel included, were vaccinated against various illnesses, some tropical, some nearer to home, and tested for venereal disease and otherwise manhandled. Some of the men fainted and were weeded out, others were perhaps too bewildered as to what was going on and saw it merely as part of a process they had to go through.

In the evenings, the men were allowed out, usually after they had taken their meal – appropriately enough in the local Zoo. Some coped better than others; many were exhausted.

From ACRC Lionel was posted to an Initial Training Wing (ITW) in Torquay (designated 5 ITW) where for twelve hours a day, seven days a week, over an eight-week period, he was given an opportunity to learn the fundamentals of Service life. He learned how to stand up straight, to march in line and to salute officers. In the classroom he studied a whole range of subjects, including such delights as hygiene and sanitation, as well as the rudiments of air force law, the principles of flight, aircraft recognition, basic navigation, armaments, and many other topics of equal fascination or drudgery. He prodded around in old engines and shot off a few rounds at the range.

Having successfully negotiated his way through ITW, Lionel expected to be on his way to an Elementary Flying Training School (EFTS) or on a ship to a far off corner of the Empire to train away from the prying eyes and the lethal guns of a deadly enemy. In the end it was the latter.

So it was that Leading Aircraftman (LAC) 1388016 Anderson, L.D., arrived in the winter of 1941 at Heaton Park in Manchester, a dreadful and dreary place that was little more than a vast and melancholy transit camp for trainees. Lionel had clearly impressed in Torquay. He was one of the few to have achieved the rank of LAC – a considerable advance from the Aircraftman (AC1) and Aircraftman Second Class (AC2) among his contemporaries. He may well have been identified as possible officer material, although that would come later.

The days were filled with parades, drills and lectures, all of which were designed to mark time while they all waited for something to happen. As one contemporary was to observe, nothing really happened at Heaton Park, as airmen simply waited to be posted. Sundays meant church parades, the men marching to the establishments of their respective faiths, the few Jews among them often sent to the kitchens to peel spuds. For them, Sunday was not a holy day. The men would spend hours outside, with their greatcoats buttoned up and their collars raised to keep out the intense cold and the rain that was typical to the north-west and that particular time of year. When excused duty they could occasionally travel into the city, where the surviving pubs (Manchester had been heavily bombed too) in the area of Piccadilly were often busier and livelier than ever.

Lionel passed much of his time thinking of home, and writing letters to his family and friends. He was concerned for his mother's health, which had recently deteriorated. His father had friends in the large Jewish community in Manchester and contacts were exchanged. They offered a welcome relief from the drab monotony of Heaton Park. In the first of many hundreds of letters that Lionel would write over the next two years, he captures the frustration and despair that he and most of his compatriots were feeling:

6th December 1941

Dear Mum, Dad and Chefsy [otherwise known as Poopela],

I've just come back from the Levy residence. Believe me Dad, one of the best things you have ever done is to send me their address. I

went to Richmond Avenue last Friday night after duty expecting to
find one of your cronies with a beard and a couple playing solo.
Gosh! What a surprise when I met Mr and Mrs Levy and their
daughter. Of course they were surprised to see me and made me
feel at home immediately. I spent the evening there with Mrs Levy
(better known to you as Dora). Their daughter Bini went out with
a soldier boy friend who is there on a week's leave. Bini asked me to
go to a football match with them Saturday afternoon. I turned up
but it was pouring with Manchester rain, so we went to town and
saw Bette Davis in the Great Lie and had tea out. We went back to
the house and spent the evening there, after having a few drinks
and some chips.

Before I left, I was once more invited there for dinner today.
I needed no second invitation and so I had a slap up dinner. As
Manchester is such a bloody awful hole, everything closes on Sunday,
so we visited Bini's grandparents whose lap I was supposed to have
wetted at some time or another. They and their auntie wish to be
remembered to you. It appears that you taught most of the
Prestwich women to play the piano dad. Anyway, if I am still in
Manchester on Tuesday (as I believe I will be), I've been invited to
Mrs Bessie Moore's (another one of your pupils) for supper. So
once more, let me thank you for that address, it certainly makes it
enjoyable for me here now as they are all so nice and lively. So
much for me.

I am sorry to hear that you are not quite better yet Mum. I do
hope you don't have another operation, so hurry up and get better
without it. By the way, let me know what size stockings you wear, so
that when I am overseas I'll probably be able to send you over a few
things like that. I must know now as my letters will be censored
before leaving this country, as things can only be sent here as
birthday presents, etc. and if you ask for them, the request will
probably be cut out by the censor.

We were issued with our sub-tropical uniforms last week. They
are light Khaki Drill material, the same design as the blue one
I have now. The badges are in red. Underneath, we wear Khaki
open-neck shirts. We have also been issued with two more sets of

underwear, a smashing pair of shoes, tropical training PT Kit and two boiler suits for mucking about with aero-engines and another kit bag, making three altogether. I didn't have to go on parade at all today, so I did not get up until 12 o'clock, this morning.

Well, I am going to have a bath and then go to bed, so cheerio once again. All my love.

Two weeks passed in Lionel's life with little or nothing to report beyond the same old routine, until at last the orders came to move. Lionel learned that he would be undertaking his training in the United States of America, a country that the day after the date of Lionel's first letter had been dramatically and finally dragged into the war following the Japanese attack on Pearl Harbor. Until then, the US had been a neutral country, but now it joined the ranks of the Allies, declaring war not only on the Japanese, but also the whole Axis of Evil. On 20 December, Lionel penned another letter home, with momentous news and another swipe at the Manchester weather:

Dear Folks,

Well, here's a bit of news. I leave Manchester tomorrow night (Sunday). Two of my kit bags are on the way to the boat now. I took them up to the camp this morning and saw them go off in a lorry this afternoon. During the morning we had a lecture by the officer (a Canadian) who will be in charge of us during the voyage. He told us that we will be spending a little while in Canada before going to the States. We were also given instruction on lifeboat drill etc. Cigarettes and Chocolates etc. will be plentiful on board at duty-free prices.

Games and Physical Training will be organised and lectures on navigation, aircraft Recognition, etc. will be held during the trip, so I don't think it will be too boring. Tomorrow morning we go to more lectures on embarkation etc. and collect our berth and cabin tickets. (I have ordered a state compartment.) By the way this officer spoke it seems as if we are going on a converted luxury liner. Well folks, there is absolutely nothing to worry about as we are going in a fairly large and fast convoy. I believe we disembark at Vancouver and then go to a place in the prairie called Moose Jaw. Well, I am all set to make the best of it and if anyone is going to have a good time from this war, it's going to be me and a few thousand others.

The weather here in Manchester the last few days has been absolutely lovely – fogs – mist – rain – frost and is always damp, but I guess I won't have to put up with it much longer. When you write in future, please address my letters to Heaton Park as they will be forwarded on to me (I hope).

I'll close now, so cheerio all. I sincerely wish you a Merry Christmas and a Prosperous and Happy New Year.

Lionel adopted an easy style to his writing, designed to reassure his anxious parents that he was, in fact, on a great adventure, rather than preparing for war, although in many ways they could be considered one and the same. By the winter of 1941/42 the dangers to shipping crossing the Atlantic were considerable. Admiral Donitz of the German Kriegsmarine (equivalent to the British Royal Navy) was building his U-boat submarine force to achieve frightening potential, and the lists of ships being sunk each month was beginning to rise.

In December 1941, the month of Lionel's departure, U-boats claimed no fewer than 28 ships destroyed but more than doubled that number the following month (66). Indeed, 1942 saw the zenith of the U-boat war, the Grand Admiral's fleet claiming some 1,322 vessels destroyed for tremendous loss of life. More importantly, perhaps, it almost brought Britain to its knees. And it was not just warships and merchantmen that were targeted. Aircraft carriers and troop ships were considered the ultimate prize, and the latter could not always rely on their speed for protection. It was at very great risk, therefore, that the convoy in which Lionel was sailing began to assemble in the Clyde.

Morning
Sunday 21st Dec 1941

Dear Folks,

Just a last line before stepping off old Blighty shore. Yes, I really am going now. We left Heaton Park 7 o'clock last night and arrived at this dock about 6 o'clock this morning. I am writing this letter on board ship. As you can understand the necessity for secrecy, I am unable to tell you where the boat is or the name of it or anything. Our quarters are quite comfortable.

My course in flying at my final destination will be two periods of nine weeks with a fortnight's leave in between. I will therefore return to England in about six months. That will give you plenty of time to get strong and healthy again Mum.

Once again, I ask you all not to worry about me – I'll be OK. In fact it is going to be a marvellous experience.

It's a damn shame about those cigarettes, but I am afraid I will not have time to enquire at the post office now. Well folks, don't forget to write to me regularly. Keep me in touch with the news, a letter means a lot when you are a couple of hundred miles from home, so I guess it will mean a hell of a lot more when the distance expands by a few thousand miles. I in turn will keep you informed of my activities at every possible chance. As I told you Mummy, if anything goes wrong at any time, I'll let you know, so when you read my letters you will know that I am not holding anything. Of course you must expect delays in between letters for the next few weeks. As soon as I get a chance on landing, I'll send you a cable-gram if I am allowed.

Sorry about Christmas. My Christmas will probably be at the sharp end of the boat leaning over the bannisters. I must pack up my kit now before going to bed.

In a different letter, written on the same day, Lionel's words managed to escape the attentions of the censor who had deleted much of his original note. Lionel and his party had in fact entrained from Manchester to Glasgow, and boarded their ship almost immediately after having left the train.

The vessel on which he travelled was a former Norwegian luxury liner, the SS *Bergensfjord*, which had been pressed into service as a troop ship. It retained its all-Norwegian crew but little or none of its pre-war elegance.

Built in 1913, she was already an old ship that had almost sunk herself in the early 1920s following an explosion in her engine room. She had been requisitioned by the British Ministry of War Transport in November 1940 and converted in Liverpool to carrying troops, undertaking her maiden voyage in her new role in February 1941. (By the end of the war she had carried some 165,000 Allied troops and sailed more than 300,000 miles.)

There was little for the airmen to do after boarding, and Lionel passed a pleasant enough hour or two after dinner watching the ship being loaded with stores. The liner finally pulled out of the dock in mid-afternoon.

Again the airmen took to the railings to watch the world go by, and were fascinated by the hulks of new ships under construction. As fast as the Glasgow dockers were making them, the Germans were sinking them, but it did not halt the all-out effort. At 17.15 hours they were ordered below decks, since it was standing orders that no men were allowed on deck after blackout hours. After tea, the men went to bed:

Christ did I say bed? We naturally sleep on hammocks. This boat is so crowded that the ceiling was one mass of hammocks, and blokes were also sleeping on mattresses on the floor. To my surprise, I went to sleep.

Tuesday 23/12/41
Reveille at 06.00 hours. I slept very well during the night. We stowed our hammocks, washed and had breakfast. We did not have to get dressed as we have to sleep in our clothes. I went up on deck at 09.15 hours (which is the earliest we can go up owing to the blackout). To my disappointment I found that we were at anchor at the mouth of the Clyde amidst dozens of other ships, presumably the convoy, then we started moving again, but we only went up and down the river and anchored again just before darkness. We were all disappointed at not moving off. There is a canteen on board which sells Players (cigarettes) at 30 for a 1/- per day. There is [sic] also chocolates etc. for sale, also canned beer. So far, I have not been sea-sick, but of course, we have only been on the calm river. We

went below decks at 17.30 (blackout time) and played cards, read and told one another dirty stories to pass the time. I went to bed with the boat still at anchor.

Wednesday 24/12/41
Woke up this morning to find the boat rocking like hell. We had moved out during the night and ran into a bit of a storm. I was mess orderly and had to get the breakfast for the whole table (14 men). As I didn't feel too good, I hardly ate any breakfast. My duties for the day as mess orderly were to dish out grub for my table, peel potatoes, sweep up and have a general clean up. The poor blokes on this ship have been sick all over the place. I have been very fortunate, I was only sick once and that was late in the afternoon. This morning, I wasn't feeling too well, but was OK again after dinner. I had something to eat for each meal and I believe that helped to pull me through. All day long the sea has been breaking over the bows of the ship and whenever I went on deck I got soaked. We are not in convoy, but have another ship with us and a destroyer on either side as escort. Our ship carries a load of machine guns and a 25lb gun on the after deck, so I guess we'll be OK. We were rather pleased at not having to carry our respirators around with us, when we received orders that life jackets have to be carried always. The grub on board is quite good. We have eight meals a day (four down and four up). This evening (Christmas Eve) we had Roast Lamb etc. This afternoon, I bought a packet of American cigarettes, called Fifth Avenue, at 6d for 20. Well, it's time to go to hammock so good night.

Thursday 25/12/41, Christmas Day
I woke up feeling fine after twelve hours sleep. The boat wasn't swaying quite so much as yesterday as the sea is much calmer. The weather isn't bad either, it's not at all cold. The Royal Marines band is aboard and they gave us a few tunes. They are going to rejoin the HMS *Warspite* which is under repair at Seattle USA. We had a very nice dinner today consisting of chicken, vegetables and some sort of sweets and some lovely apples. I had half a pint of beer as well. Christmas Day has been really rather dull as a whole, but I must be

thankful that I have been well. I have just bought some Cadbury's
Whole Nut milk chocolate, the first I've seen for months. Well, once
more, I turn in, with a bright moon shining on a fairly calm sea.

Many of the items that Lionel mentions would have been rare treats for
an Englishman living at home, where rationing meant that food such as
chocolate was a luxury. His specific mention of HMS *Warspite* is similarly worthy of note. The Grand Old Lady, as she was known, had arrived
in the US in August 1941 after an epic journey through the Suez Canal
and across the Indian Ocean. A refit at Puget Sound Naval Shipyard
included replacing her main armament and significantly upgrading her
anti-aircraft defences. She was recommissioned on 28 December.

As the days progressed the airmen became more accustomed to the ship,
and less inclined to be seasick. But the North Atlantic was no place to
be in a gale, the only positive to be seen was that foul weather made a
U-boat attack less likely:

Friday 26/12/41
Woke up this morning to find the ship tossing about like a cork in a
lavatory. The sea was pretty rough all day. The swaying of the ship
had no effect on me at all. Life on board went on as usual, eat,
drink, nosh, go up on deck and get wet, etc. and played cards before
supper. The grub is quite good and I eat plenty of it as the sea air
seems to give me quite an appetite. The name of the ship by the way
is HMS [sic] *Bergensfjord*. I believe it was originally used for trans-
porting cattle, but what's the difference between troops and cattle?

Saturday 27/12/41
Things went on as usual today. The sea has been getting rougher
all day. The ship was tossing about quite a bit when I went below
for supper. We had some good old Yiddisher Fried Fish for supper.
These Norwegian cooks sure know how to cook. I had a haircut
today; one of the marines did it for me. Rumours have just come
round that we were chased by submarines last night and the night
before. The engines of the other ship that is accompanying us broke

down today owing to the fact that they were overstrained when the ships were scooting away from the submarines. One of the chaps said that he doesn't care if this boat is sunk as it doesn't belong to him. I was mess orderly once again which entails quite a bit of work. Nothing else unusual happened. The sea was much calmer and it was very much colder.

Sunday 28/12/41
The sea has been pretty rough all day and it's been freezing cold, a sure sign that we are drawing near Canadian shores. A welcome sight which also caused a bit of excitement was an aircraft of the Royal Canadian Air Force, which flew over and around us. I handed in six £1 notes which will go to my credit at my next station in America. I'll certainly be glad to be on dry land again. This voyage has been no pleasure. We are cramped for comfort and I am very bored with doing nothing for a week. All I've seen has been sea, and more bloody sea. But for all that we make our own fun and make the best of it.

Monday 29/12/41
All I can say for today is that it has been a bitterly cold atmosphere. I don't think I have ever been in such a cold atmosphere before. We were expecting to dock tonight, but as no land has been sighted yet, I don't suppose we will be in before tomorrow or Thursday. We are all feeling sore at having to spend New Year's Eve on this crate as well as Christmas.

Wednesday 31/12/41, New Year's Eve
We are due to dock tomorrow thank heaven. As it is New Year's Eve, the 14 blokes on our table pooled all our spare cash (as only £1 and 10/- notes could be changed into Canadian money) and bought as much beer as we could. We had a sing-song and quite a few drinks as a celebration. At 19.00 hours (which is midnight in England), we gave a toast to 'The Folks at Home' and to the 'Armies who had gone before us'. We were all thinking of our families back home.

The journey had been far from a pleasure cruise. The crossing had been rough, although not as much as the Atlantic could have been, and the airmen had had to fight the dual enemies of fear and boredom, one feeding the other.

As they approached the Canadian shores, they had the comfort of coming under the protection of the RCAF, whose aircraft would significantly help to deter a U-boat attack. No U-boat dared be caught on the surface, and yet submerged they could not travel fast enough to keep pace with the convoy.

The airmen were impatient to step ashore, to be once again on dry land. But perhaps they might not have been in such a rush if they knew what was to follow. Yet anything was better than being tossed about in their Norwegian tub, and it was with blessed relief that the ship finally came into dock at Halifax, Nova Scotia, a freezing town on a freezing day.

Once again the RAF did not delay. The troops were not to enjoy the luxuries of their new berth, such as they were, but rather they were formed into ranks and marched straight to a waiting train belonging to the Canadian National Railway. The faithful steam engine was ready to transport them the 300 miles to a town in New Brunswick called Moncton, a journey of some five and a half hours.

After the relentless and featureless drudgery of the sea, the landscape that confronted them was close to Utopia. Although the train travelled throughout the night, the moon was bright enough for the men to be able to pick out the most marvellous scenery imaginable: deep valleys of enormous pines, breathtaking in their sheer size and scale, all covered in glistening snow; and great lakes covered in ice.

Moncton was home to 31 RAF Depot (formerly 31 Personnel Depot) and had only been formed a few weeks before Lionel and his party arrived. Although the facilities at Moncton would later be developed and include a flying training establishment, the site was little more than a holding camp, accommodating the men prior to their onward journey to the United States. It allowed Lionel plenty of time to explore, and he liked what he saw and who he met:

Moncton is a small town 700 miles from the nearest big city which is Montreal. The main street at night is one blaze of lights and signs. Nearly everyone has a car and boy what cars. I was given a lift back to camp in one last night. The people here are very nice and are willing to help whenever they can. Things are very strange, what with the currency, traffic going on the wrong side of the road, the different expressions they use, etc. The cost of living is terribly high as there are about four different taxes on practically everything you buy. There is not a single pub here at all, the only place you can get a drink is from a bootlegger and that's illegal so we steer clear.

He was also impressed with the camp, and especially the food:

We are stationed at an ultra modern camp which is about a third of the size of the town. We have comfortable double tier beds, hot and cold showers, modern wash basins and central heating. The food is simply marvellous. I had roast beef and fried tomatoes, porridge, and as much bread and butter and jam as I want. This is the first time the RAF has dished up a really good cup of tea. Fruit is plentiful and the best. I actually had a banana yesterday. So you see I am having a pretty good time out here.

Lionel also found an ingenious way of communicating with his family, via 'airgraph' – effectively miniaturised letters, copied and reproduced on a piece of paper measuring but a few square inches. To make use of an aerograph, however, the recipient had to be in military service. He explains this in a cryptic note at the end of his letter to his parents of 3 January:

PS. The cockeyed address on airgraph [sic] is because I can only send it to people in the forces. How do you like army life, Private Abrahams?!

The men were immediately taken into the heart of the local community, and began to recognise that although they may have spoken the same language as their Canadian hosts, they were otherwise entirely different people, at least culturally. Even the etiquette at a dance left Lionel wondering whether he would ever feel entirely at home:

Well, I've been in Canada nearly a week and I've enjoyed every
moment of it. Most of my dollars have been spent on ices, banana
splits, apple pies and whipped cream, milk shakes by the dozen.
There is no shortage of anything here.

I went to a dance again last night and had rather an enjoyable
evening. I am gradually getting into the Canadian style of dancing
which is simply ghastly. The girls put their arm around your neck
and stick their behind out and then do a cross between a jitter-bug
and a route march. They have strange customs as regards dances,
etc. For instance, to ask a girl for a dance without first being
introduced is simply not done. The girl feels hurt if the boy doesn't
clap after a dance as he is supposed to clap for her. One of the girls
told me that Moncton was once known as the city of girls, but the
RAF has changed all that. There are not enough of them now.

I went to the pictures the night before last and saw Merle Oberon
in 'Dydea'. I was surprised to see a notice forbidding smoking.
They don't have continuous shows, but two or three shows a day.
The admission is 10 cents and 20 cents but when the tax is added it
costs 32 cents and 45 cents .

The YMCA got me an invitation out for supper tonight. The
man, Mr Daly, is going to pick me up in his car outside the camp
this evening. I'll probably suffer from air sickness as I am eating
all the time. We had tea in the camp and then went into town. The
first place we visited was Dickens' Grill Room, where we had a milk
shake. Then we popped into the YMCA for a few games of table
tennis. We left there and went back to the Grill Room (Milk Bar
in England) and had hamburgers, apple-pie with large lumps of
whipped cream and ice-cream and washed it down with coffee.
We went to the pictures and returned later for a Banana Royal.

Lionel promised to send home some of the luxuries that he was currently
enjoying, although he thought it unlikely he would get the chance until
he had arrived at a more permanent posting. While he waited his turn,
groups of men were entrained for various parts of the US: Texas, Florida,
Oklahoma, Arizona, California and Hollywood. Lionel learned that he
was destined for Florida or Arizona, and either would be welcome to

escape the Canadian winter. In the event, his posting to Arizona was confirmed, but he was not in any great rush – not when there appeared to be a steady stream of luxury food and girls on tap:

How is your health now Mum? As for myself, I don't think I have ever felt or looked fitter. This 'XX' cold climate seems to agree with me. Although the sun is not strong here, I look as if I've been sun-bathing. However, I will soon have to put up with the boiling hot sun as I have been posted from here to Arizona (the land of cowboys and Indians). I leave Moncton next Sunday on a five or six day train journey which will take me some 2,000 miles. I am rather looking forward to it as it will be an entirely new experience.

So far I have had a marvellous time here. I have been invited out quite a few times with a pal of mine to people's houses for tea and supper. One man drove us out to a place called Magnetic Hill which is supposed to oppose Newton's Law of Gravity. We drove down the hill in his car, released the brakes at the bottom of the hill and free-wheeled up the hill. It has got me puzzled. He then took us home and we had a smashing supper. I only wish that you in England could get all the stuff that is available here. Better still, I wish you were all here.

The other night this same friend of mine and myself were walk-ing along the main street when a couple of sleighs pulled by a couple of horses and full up with about twenty girls whizzed past us. The girls called to us to jump on. Needless to say, we did. The sleighs took us all round town picking up fellows all the time and finally pulled up outside a church hall where we spent the evening playing games, dancing and eating hot dogs which were washed down with cocoa. We had a really enjoyable evening. We went to Church one Sunday and were invited to supper by one of the women there (and her two daughters). Once more we enjoyed our-selves, so you see I am being well looked after in Canada and it is just like a marvellous holiday. Next week will see me on my way to the States where I really start to work. It is a hard course, lasting about 20 weeks. I have been told that the hospitality in the States is even better than it is here.

Lionel's excitement at the prospect of flying instruction was tempered by an understandable anxiety as to whether he would make the grade. Moncton, as well as being a receiving centre for those about to embark on their pilot training, was also a camp for those who had failed, and were awaiting their fate. The number of those with their 'wings and tapes' (ie flying brevet and badges of rank) seemed to be in equal proportion to those with the abject look of a star player dropped from the 1st XV, and Lionel reckoned his chances of success were no better than 50:50.

His last letter to his parents was written on 15 January and it was to be a full week before Lionel was able to write to them again – a week in which he and a group of around fifty trainee pilots had embarked on an epic journey across Canada and the US, causing a sensation at every railway station and in every city they stayed. They passed through the provinces of New Brunswick, Nova Scotia and Quebec, all covered in snow. Then they journeyed through the states of Illinois, Iowa, Kansas, Texas, New Mexico, Missouri and Oklahoma, until finally arriving in Arizona:

Our first stop was at Montreal where we had to change from the Canadian National Railway to the Canadian Pacific. We had four hours to spend after we had our lunch at the Station buffet, so four of us hired a taxi and toured the city for about two and a half hours. The taxi driver was a French Canadian and was a perfect guide. We saw a most marvellous Cathedral called Notre Dame, a very modern Jewish Hospital, German Internment Camp, St Lawrence River, and the largest Drug Store in the world, with self-opening doors. He took us to the slums and the rich quarters and practically all the places of interest in Montreal. It was really worth the $5 we paid him.

The next stop was Toronto for half an hour to pick up customs officials. It was dark when we arrived there, so we did not see much of it. Eight o'clock Tuesday morning we stopped at Chicago. As soon as people saw the Great Britain label we wear on our shoulders they fell for us. Some of our chaps were given cigarettes and chocolate, etc. We had breakfast on the station and hopped into a fleet of taxis which were waiting to take us to another train on the other part of the city. We had an hour to wait there, so we made a dash for the nearest sky-scraper, which was the Board of Trade Building and took a lift to the 43rd floor. It was really marvellous up there. I could see practically the whole of the city. I took some photographs up there.

On our way back to the station, a Chicago Cop gave me a big box of chewing gum. People would have done anything for us. We left Chicago on the Golden State train at 10.15 Tuesday morning. On the train we met some American chaps who were going to San Diego and join the US Marines and some others who were going to another Flying Field in Arizona. There were also civilians on the train who were very interesting to talk to and who insisted in buying us drinks, etc. This train took us all the way from Chicago to Mesa – Arizona. The scenery was really marvellous. We saw the Rocky Mountains, some picturesque canyons, and large flat prairie lands. I just can't put it all into words.

Lionel at Mesa.

Chapter 2

Home from Home

After four days and four nights of travelling, the train finally pulled into the station at Mesa, a small town near Phoenix. Two coaches were there to greet them and drive them along roads adorned with orange groves to their new home, officially designated 4 British Flying Training School (4 BFTS).

> The aerodrome is only seven months old. Our billets are air conditioned. We have marvellous beds, writing desks and armchairs. There are football pitches, tennis courts and games rooms, etc. We also have a magnificent lounge and canteen. The lounge is more like a hotel lounge and the canteen is like a first class milk bar.
>
> Looking out of my bedroom window, I can see some of the most marvellous scenery. I can see the front of one of the hangers [sic] with some yellow and blue training planes standing on the tarmac. By the side of that is the runway where planes are landing and taking off all day long. Behind all this is a background of mountains. The colouring is too beautiful to explain.
>
> Our food is the best anyone can expect. It is served up to us by waiters and we can have as much as we like. Breakfast this morning consisted of eggs, bread and butter and marmalade, half pint milk and coffee with cream. Dinner was fish and chips and salad, followed by peaches and cream, and tea which is called supper is steak and potatoes and lettuce. We have coffee and cream and half pint of milk with every meal.

The British Flying Training School at Mesa was indeed a new facility, one of seven schools that would eventually be created in the US, from Clewiston, Florida, in the east to the appropriately named Lancaster, California, on the west coast. The rationale for training RAF pilots overseas (facilities were chosen in South Africa, Rhodesia and Canada as well as the US) was a simple one: the virtually guaranteed decent weather, wide open spaces and complete absence of an enemy air force provided a safer and more efficient environment in which to turn fledglings into eagles.

The first cadets arrived in September 1941, a few months before the Americans entered the war, and wore civilian rather than military clothes. The training school at Mesa had a nucleus of RAF staff comprising a commanding officer, administrative officer and a handful of non-commissioned officers (NCOs) with responsibility for armaments, signals and other specialist training. In charge of organisation from the outset were Squadron Leader Bill Holloway and Squadron Leader Stuart Mills, the former becoming the school's first commanding officer (despite not being a pilot) and the latter staying briefly as the chief flying instructor (CFI).

Mills had already been through an eventful war, having been awarded the Distinguished Flying Cross (DFC) as a fighter pilot with 263 Squadron during the campaign in Norway in April 1940. He was wounded in May, the spell in hospital saving his life in more ways than one. His fellow pilots embarked on the aircraft carrier *Glorious* to return to the UK, and nearly all were lost when she was sunk by the German capital ship *Scharnhorst*. When recovered, Mills assumed command of 87 Squadron at the height of the Battle of Britain, before being posted to the US in December 1940 as an assistant air attaché with a brief to help develop British training facilities.

All of the principal instructors, ground staff and supporting staff were American civilians, the instructors being addressed by their surnames at all times. At 4 BFTS, these included a core of men from Southwest Airways, an airline that had chosen Mesa as one of three airfields from which to deliver its service. Southwest Airways had been the brainchild of Hollywood producer Leland Hayward and pilot John H. Connelly, who had created the airline with the support of a number of major Hollywood actors of the time. The airfield at Mesa was originally to have been called Thunderbird Field III but, the story goes, the RAF insisted on the name 'Falcon' and so the airfield became Falcon Field.

Training was similar at every BFTS, comprising twenty-eight weeks in three parts: 'primary' training was on the Stearman PT13; 'basic' training progressed to the Vultee BT13; and 'advanced' was completed on the North American AT6A 'Harvard'. Lionel was excited about what the future had in store, and the reception they had so far received:

Although we have arrived in the middle of an Arizona Winter the weather is just like an English summer. We wear Khaki shirts and trousers and no tunic on the 'drome, but we change into our Blue when we go out. There are no corporals, etc. here, but two RAF Officers and one sergeant. They are all decent chaps. Our course has been extended to 28 weeks, so don't expect me home for a while.

I trust all is well at home. I wish you could all be here with me instead of London and its air-raids, blackouts, rationing, etc., The Americans really do think a lot of the British. One woman in the train told me that she really gets a thrill when she talks to us boys. I got a thrill when she paid for my sherry and asked if I would like another.

The hospitality of the people here is simply terrific. If I was to walk into a hotel, about a dozen chaps will ask me to have a drink. One chap has already invited me to his home in San Francisco when I have my leave here. I don't think I'll go there though because if I have not been failed in nine weeks' time I will probably go to Los Angeles.

Lionel was also quick to extend his contacts within the local Jewish community:

Whilst the rest of my flight is at church, I'll tell you what I did yesterday. Our sergeant called me into his office and gave me the name and phone number of a Jewish girl in Phoenix. She had constantly asked him if there were any Jewish chaps here. I am the first Yid to fly in Arizona so he gave her my name. Well, I phoned her and arranged to meet her in town with a friend of mine here

Jack Anderson (no relation as you probably know). We hitch-hiked
the 28 miles into Phoenix where we met her and a Jewish girl
friend. She took us home where her mother turned out a delicious
supper, after which we borrowed her mother's car and drove into
town again and boy, did we have a grand time. We looked all over
town and ended up in a very select night-club. Privates in the army
are not allowed in here, only officers, and air cadets. After that, the
girls drove us back to our Field or Aerodrome. I have a permanent
invitation to the house of Mr and Mrs Nover. The girl's name is
Elaine.

After a false dawn, and the need for further ground instruction on the
aircraft he was destined to fly, Lionel finally received the news he wanted
to hear. On 28 January he was kitted out with a parachute pack and introduced to his flying instructor, Larry Mills (always referred to as 'Mr
Mills'), and his aircraft:

Well at long last I have been 'upstairs'. I took off yesterday for the
first time and it was grand. I started on aerobatics today. From now
on I go up for about 45 minutes to an hour each day. So far my
instructor is very pleased with me. I have not suffered any ill effects
such as air-sickness.

The aircraft that Lionel flew was a Boeing Stearman PT13, the US
equivalent of the ubiquitous De Havilland DH82, better known as the
Tiger Moth. The two aircraft shared several similarities: both were
biplanes that would not have looked much out of place in the First World
War; both took their first flights in the early 1930s, just as the biplane was
fast becoming obsolete; and both became the chief primary training aircraft of their respective nations.

   As a primary training aircraft, the Stearman was close to perfection. Its
120hp Continental engine provided a maximum speed of up to 126mph,
and the aircraft could climb at a rate of 840ft per minute to a maximum
ceiling of 11,200ft. Most important of all, she was a stable and forgiving
aircraft, even in the hands of a novice pilot, and yet could perform aerobatics like a modern-day stunt plane. She was also beautifully presented,

with a green/blue fuselage, bright yellow wings and striped red and white rudder.

Primary training necessitated the trainee pilot to undertake around ten hours of dual instruction, where he would learn how to take off and land, and perform gentle banks and turns until such time as the instructor was confident that he could leave his charge to fly a solo circuit of the airfield and land without breaking his neck or, more importantly, the aircraft.

Accidents did, of course, happen, the most common being a 'ground loop', with the aircraft landing on its back. As the dual hours mounted, the trainees would become increasingly nervous, and there was a healthy rivalry to see who would be the first to fly solo. For some, that time would never come. On Friday 13 February, Lionel wrote a long letter to his parents, sharing the thrills and spills of the previous few days and explaining the context of a steady flow of photographs that he was now sending home:

Today is Friday the 13th and it sure is my unlucky day. I should really have started to fly solo today, but owing to the fact that my instructor was away, I have not been able to complete my ten hours dual. However, I will probably have my first solo flight next Tuesday (I hope). Today was unlucky for a couple of other chaps in my flight who had their first solo flight as they both did a ground loop (ask any pilot what that is). All they did was to scrape their wing tips on the ground and give themselves a hell of a scare. As ground loops are quite frequent, we had an agreement that the first bloke in our flight who did one would buy drinks all round, so it has cost them quite a bit.

I have only one photograph this week which will be of any interest to you. It was taken by one of my pals as I was walking back to the crew room with my instructor after a flight. The straps etc. on me is [sic] for the parachute. I get on very well with my instructor and he may take me to Los Angeles in his car in the near future for a weekend.

He also took the opportunity to chide his father over the incident that came to be known as 'The Channel Dash', where three German warships – the *Scharnhorst*, *Gneisenau* and *Prinz Eugen* – broke out of the French port of Brest in a bid to take refuge in their home ports in Germany. Despite the heroic if somewhat chaotic response from the RAF and Fleet Air Arm (FAA) under the codename 'Operation Fuller', the warships managed to make the journey virtually unmolested:

> What do you think of the news? Really Dad, you shouldn't have let those German battleships go through the Straits of Dover like that. At the time of writing, Singapore is still holding out. I hope they keep it up. The morale in America is very high. As is traditional, the average American believes that now the States are in the war, it will be over in six months. Of course, we British boys have to be very diplomatic and agree with them. They admire the British very much for standing up to the air-raids as we have done.

While his instructor was away, Lionel studied hard: meteorology; navigation; signals; engines; principles of flight; instruments; airmanship; and aircraft recognition. But it was certainly not all work and no play. A visiting rodeo, midget car racing, and the thought of a party at a local girls' college provided welcome distraction:

> Saturday afternoon and saw a very unusual and enjoyable show as well as thrilling. If you don't know what a Rodeo is, it's a competition between a load of cowboys in trick horse riding – steer wrestling, wild cow milking, riding bareback, bucking broncos, etc. I had a weekend pass, so I went to a night club with one of our chaps and a couple of American soldiers. The place was called the Die Dahoni Club. I was there until about 1.30 in the morning. Sunday was spent at the midget car races. Next Sunday ought to prove interesting as 50 of us have been invited to a party at Temple Girls College. Temple is a small town about twelve miles from here.

Lionel's turn to fly solo came on 20 February:

> I took a plane up solo today. I was practicing [sic] landings and take

offs on the aerodrome today with my instructor. When he got out
of the cockpit and said: 'OK Anderson. You take it up and land it in
one piece', boy, was I surprised and pleased. I opened the throttle
and took off. I climbed up to 700 feet and while I circled the aerodrome, I realized that I had to land the ship myself and my landings
were not exactly perfect. However, I closed the throttle and put the
bus in a nice gentle glide. For the first time I did everything right
and came down in one of the best landings I have ever made. It was
so smooth that I was really surprised to find myself on the ground.

My instructor came running over to me grinning all over his
face, shook my hand and said: 'Congratulations Pilot, now do it
again.' I did [it] three times and took off and landed solo. I felt very
pleased with myself and it's really marvellous to be up there all by
myself. I was singing all the time. So your son is now a pilot (sort of).

Very quickly, Lionel's flying experience began to mount, but there was
a thin dividing line between confidence and overconfidence, and although
the Stearman was forgiving, she could not entirely be taken for granted.
At the time of writing his next letter, he was in the middle of what he
jokingly described as the Arizona rainy season – a downpour that lasted
three hours but only happened three or four times a year:

In one of my previous letters, I told you about some chaps in my
flight, ground looping. Well, this morning I was up solo for an hour.
I came in and landed OK, looked at my watch and decided that I
had enough time to fly round the aerodrome, so I took off again
and when I came in to land the second time, I lost altitude in a
perfect glide and when my wheels touched the ground, everything
went haywire, my left wing went down and hit the ground, the aircraft veered off to the right and suddenly swung round to face the
opposite way and stopped, so that is a ground loop. I damaged the
wing a little when it hit and scraped along the ground. I am OK
myself, the only thing I felt was wild. My instructor saw me do it and
burst out laughing when I got back to him, and it has cost me two
dollars in drinks for the boys. Apart from this incident today, my
flying isn't too bad. I have four and a half hours solo to my credit.

I received a letter from one of my pals who is now in a Training School in Florida (100 miles from Miami Beach). He tells me that out of the nine chaps of our old Torquay 'D' Flight who went to Canada – six of them have failed. I have also heard of several other D Flight chaps who have also failed.

The dangers on base were not only restricted to flying:

We have been warned about Black Widow Spiders, Scorpions and Rattle Snakes which will be in abundance in the desert surrounding our 'drome in the coming summer months. We are advised to tap our boots on the floor in the morning and look in our beds at night before getting into them. Sounds good doesn't it! But I don't think they will worry us too much (I hope).

While having tea one afternoon, a funny thing happened in the Mess involving a snake:

I was eating at one end of the Mess Hall when there was a sudden commotion down the other end. A load of the boys suddenly got up and stood on tables and chairs, like a load of women who had just spotted a mouse. The cause of the commotion was a three foot long snake, which the station doctor had slipped in for a joke. We did not know that it was not poisonous. The funny part was that fifty brave British Airmen were standing on chairs and tables while a fourteen year old mess waiter calmly picked it up by the tail and threw it out. That's life in Arizona for you.

Not every encounter with the snakes, however, was so amusing:

One of the Mexican gardeners was nearly bitten by it while he was cutting the lawn outside our billets. We expect hundreds of the b----y things here now.

Letters to and from home were vital to maintaining morale, but Lionel's epic journey from a cold, damp and miserable Manchester holding camp to the hot, dry and exciting Arizona desert via a freezing Nova Scotia, where he suffered from frostbitten ears after someone had made off with his scarf, meant that correspondence often went astray, or took weeks and sometimes even months to catch up. It caused considerable frustration on all sides.

On at least one occasion, Lionel received four letters in a day, not only from his parents but also from other relatives and friends. His younger brother, Gerald, would also write, telling him of his own adventures at home and progress at school, and even once volunteering to knit Lionel a new pullover – perhaps unaware that his brother had swapped the 45 degrees below zero chill of Canada for the baking hot sands of the American desert. Despite the beauty of the surrounding area, he clearly missed home, and the comfort of rituals and cultures that were more familiar:

The scenery in Arizona has its own particular type of beautiful scenery. High mountains all round, some of which are a beautiful reddish colour. The desert here is covered in shrubs and about 300 different varieties of cactus. But I still like the good old English Countryside. When you get out here, you realise how green England is.

The buildings are very much different to the ones at home. In the towns, Phoenix for instance, the centre is full of hotels, shops, casinos, etc. all of which are white. There are one or two tall buildings about 14 storeys. Around the centre you have the residential area. The majority of houses are bungalows and are white or of some light colour. The streets are all wide and look very picturesque with the palm trees on either side.

As far as dress goes, I guess you know how flashily the Americans dress. The town men are dressed something like this: White trilby hat – Red jacket – green trousers – brown and white shoes – pink shirt and red and green tie – and that is not exaggerated. There are several Stetsons and riding boots with spurs to be seen as well. The women dress mainly in sports dresses, etc. A couple of weeks ago however when the Rodeo was in town, everyone dressed up in very colourful cowboy dress.

The customs vary quite a bit from ours and I haven't got enough paper to write them all down. The first thing you do when you get into town is to have your shoes cleaned by a negro boy for a nickel (3d). Tips get me. Wherever you go you have to leave a tip. Another thing is that the Americans at meals cut everything up first and then eat with the forks only.

As for the home life, I have been home with quite a few people, some of them are very formal and others are very lively and make you feel right at home. The children are usually out on dates if they are over 14 or 15. A girl here doesn't think she is popular unless she has about 10 dates a week. Don't expect me to write an article to the 'Willesden Chronicle', but I guess you have enough information to compose one of your own.

Joe Anderson did indeed have sufficient material to make up his own article, though he chose a different approach with his local newspaper. Lionel's father was well known to the *Willesden Chronicle's* editor, and therefore sent regular batches of correspondence to the paper about his son's adventures. Many of these letters appeared word for word, including news of Lionel's first solo, which appeared under the headline: 'Neasden Airman in America'.

The propaganda value of such correspondence is difficult to gauge, but talk of the exciting life that Lionel and his friends were experiencing must have been a welcome distraction from the bombing and the Blitz, and in recognising that there was another life outside London and outside the UK.

As well as hard print, there was also the wonder of radio. Having completed his solo flight, Lionel was invited into a local studio to broadcast home, and was the voice at the beginning to declare: 'This is the Royal Air Force calling England.' He did not think the voice sounded much like his, but was clearly excited about the prospect of his parents hearing him from thousands of miles away.

The weather, which Lionel refers to frequently in his letters, was not always benign. He had spent a pleasant few days during Passover with his friends, the Novers, and their daughter, thanks to the generosity of

the RAF contingent's commanding officer who had permitted him
leave of absence to celebrate the Jewish festival. He had by now been at
Mesa for six weeks and had thirty hours of flying under his belt, and
was expecting to start night flying on his next trip 'upstairs'. Some of his
group had failed to make the grade – a danger to themselves and others
– and been 'washed out' in American parlance. Lionel was studying for
a new set of exams when the weather closed in:

Well, I have just had a new experience. This afternoon, flying was
suspended owing to a very strong wind. As the afternoon went on,
the wind gradually strengthened until there was a fairly strong gale
blowing. By six o'clock this evening a hurricane was in force. The
sand from the desert was blowing all over the place. A couple of
doors were blown off their hinges and sand was blown in all over
our beds and on the floor. In fact the whole place was covered in
sand. It lasted for about three hours.

I went over to the canteen for a cup of coffee and had to wear my
helmet and goggles and a handkerchief over my mouth to get there.
It finally subdued and we have just finished clearing some of the
sand out of our beds so that we can get some sleep tonight. So I
have now had the experience of being in a hurricane.

The following day dawned bright and sunny, and it was a case of all hands
making light work of the clearing up. The sand was everywhere – in the
beds, in the cupboards, in their clothes and in their food – and it was to
take several days until the place was thoroughly clean again. When he
wasn't lending a hand with the dustpan and brush, Lionel wrote in detail
about his flying experiences:

I have some time to spare so I will write a bit about flying and what
it is like. As you know, I take a plane up solo every day now. The
first time I was allowed to go away from the 'drome to do some
exercises I tried to do a loop. I went up 5,000 feet so that I should
have plenty of height. I put the plane in a dive and pulled up to
start the loop. The next thing I knew was that I was upside down
and dangling from my safety belt. I was quite surprised and to be

truthful, a little alarmed. It took me quite a few seconds to figure a way out of it.

Some of the exercises we have to do are: Loops – Spins – Stalls – Various degree turns – co-ordination – 8's – S turns etc. This may sound like double dutch to you, but if you ask anybody who knows anything about flying, they will explain them to you. Some of these manoeuvres made me quite dizzy at first. However, I am quite used to them now and like them very much. So far, I have not been sick.

I believe one of the hardest things to get used to is inverted flying. All I have is a strap going across my thighs to hold me in. When I am upside down I can feel myself leave the seat and dangle about two or three inches from it. When you look up and see the ground about 4,000 feet away it is very comforting to know that your parachute is on. However, I am quite used to that now and rather like it.

Spins used to make my stomach hit the roof of my mouth as the plane is spinning round and round and diving at the same time. When you look at the ground it seems to be flying around in all directions. After doing these a few times, I am able to pull the plane out of a spin just where and when I want to (sort of).

My instructor (Mr Mills) is a bit of a lad. Sometimes while we are up there he says: 'OK Anderson, is your safety strap done up?' When I've checked it, he will then say: 'Right. Take a couple of deep breaths and relax.' Then everything goes haywire for about five minutes. After that he looks in the mirror and grins at me. I have got to the stage now, when I can grin back at him. It is really grand fun though. When you come to think of it, it costs Americans hundreds of dollars to learn to fly at a place like this and we are getting paid to do it.

The excitement of flying was punctuated by excursions off site. Teas and dances were organised by the local British War Relief Society, who also arranged for parcels to be sent home to England. Lionel endeavoured to send his mother some lemons.

And there was another distraction, one of enormous future significance. And it involved the movies.

Preston Foster, the Hollywood 'star' of *Thunder Birds*.

Chapter 3

Thunder Birds

For some weeks a large party of moviemakers from 20th Century Fox had established themselves on the airfield in preparation for making a new film, whose title was to have far-reaching consequences on the Anderson household. The film was entitled: *Thunder Birds – Soldiers of the Air*.

> Tomorrow Jean Tierney [sic] and Preston Foster come here to make a film called 'Thunderbird' [sic]. They shot a couple of scenes a few weeks ago, but I believe they start on the job properly tomorrow. We will be photographed going through our normal daily routine as a background to the film.

The crew was in fact on 'set' for more than three weeks with their enormous arc lamps, cameras, clapperboards and other such paraphernalia. The RAF contingent, along with a group of American airmen and a similar group of Chinese cadets brought in for the purpose, were used throughout the film, but especially in the opening sequences, the RAF marching past the camera in their best blue.

The story revolves around Steve Britt, a civilian flying instructor (Foster) who is training Peter Stackhouse (John Sutton), a young RAF cadet, to fly. Both men inevitably fall for the same girl (Tierney). The cadet is driven to join the RAF to avenge his brother, killed in an early raid on Wilhemshaven, and his instructor is equally determined to see that he makes the grade, despite his pupil suffering severe air sickness.

A film that is unashamedly produced and directed with its propaganda value uppermost in mind, it includes a scene where Stackhouse's grandmother writes to Winston Churchill, enclosing a cheque for £25,000 to buy a bomber for the Germans to receive an immediate reply. It is a direct homage to the very real example of Lady Rachel Workman MacRobert who lost her three sons to flying accidents or enemy action. When her youngest son, Iain, was reported missing, she made a donation of £25,000 to purchase a bomber for the RAF and asked that it be named *MacRobert's Reply*. (A succession of RAF aircraft still carry the name today.)

The film's director, William A. Wellman, was in constant attendance, as were many of the actors. Preston Foster was a 'he man' actor very much in the mould of Errol Flynn, right down to his pencil-thin moustache. Arguably he was a more diverse talent, having starred on Broadway before moving into films in 1929. His leading lady, Gene Tierney, was a different class altogether, having been educated at the finest schools on the east coast and at a finishing school in Switzerland. Nicknamed 'The Get Girl', she shared a love of Broadway with her co-star, but any further similarities started and ended there. She was only twenty-two when she started filming *Thunder Birds*.

Foster's love rival in the film, John Sutton, was different again, a classic product of the Empire and the British public school system. He was a technical consultant, working in the film industry, when he was effectively 'spotted' and offered a role in *The Last of the Mohicans*, alongside Randolph Scott. He had worked with Gene Tierney previously in *Hudson's Bay*.

Among the supporting cast, perhaps the most appropriate given the subject matter, was Reginald Denny who took the part of Squadron Leader Barrett, the senior RAF officer. He had been a pilot in the Royal Flying Corps, the forerunner to the RAF, for two years and brought his acting and flying experiences to Hollywood, working in several films as a stunt pilot. He was also interested in model aircraft and invented a radio-controlled target drone, delivering a better and safer way of training anti-aircraft gunners.

The filming, and the concept of a flying training school, also served as a magnet for other major 'stars':

I have already written to tell you about the film we have been making here. It has helped me to meet a few celebrities. We have practically finished. It is in technicolor and will be showing in a couple of months. I don't know how long it will take to reach England, but when it does, be sure to see it. Ralph and Preston (my pals) are quite decent chaps and we have had an interesting conversation.

I am in quite a few of the crowd scenes or rather marching scenes. Besides me, Jack Holt (an American Army Officer), Reginald Denny (an RAF Officer), Preston Foster (a civilian in love with Gene Tierney) and John Sutton (an RAF Cadet) are in it. There are quite a few extras, camera men, electricians and whatnots hanging around.

Joan Fontaine and Brian Aherne were here a couple of days ago. I danced with Joan Fontaine at the graduation dance last Thursday. I like her. There is no swank about her and she is rather attractive. She wasn't all dressed up, but dressed like any other human being. The only snag was that while I danced with her, her old man kept his eyes on her. She dances very nicely. Nearly as well as me! So you see I am meeting quite a few celebrities here. Gracie Fields is coming to Phoenix next week and will probably come over here to our 'drome.

Joan Fontaine was something of a beauty. Fontaine was her stage name; she was born Joan de Beauvoir de Havilland, the younger sister of Olivia de Havilland and a near relative of Geoffrey de Havilland, the founder of the aircraft manufacturer that bore his name and whose arguably greatest creation Lionel would ultimately fly in combat. As an actress she was at the height of her powers, having only recently been given an Academy Award for Best Actress for her role in the Alfred Hitchcock thriller, *Suspicion*. She had married Brian Aherne, himself an Oscar-nominated British actor, in 1939.

Gracie Fields did indeed put on a show, organised through the good auspices of the British War Relief Society, and Lionel went as a guest of Dick and Libby McGuire, two stalwarts of the Society whom 'Andy' (as they called him) had befriended:

We were picked up there by some very good friends of ours, Mr &

Mrs McGuire who took us home to a turkey dinner. After partaking
of this delicious meal, they then took us to the Phoenix Union High
School to see Gracie Fields. This school as many other American
schools has a theatre arrangement about the size of the Odeon
(Craven Park). They have a lovely stage and two British Cadets
from Falcon Field plonked Gracie right in the middle of it (one of
the boys comes from Rochdale). She put over a marvellous show.

For about two and a half hours (except for a short inter-mission
in which I went out to wash my hands) she just sang. I think I can
say that I have never enjoyed a show as I did that one. She was here
last year and the Americans really do like her. During the program
[sic] she told them something about what is going on in England
today. I won't tell you what does go on as you probably know. She
came up to our Camp on Sunday and gave our boys a show all to
themselves. Some of us have her Los Angeles address and [she]
want[s] us to look her up when we get our leave.

After the show we went home with the McGuires for the night as
we had weekend passes. I arose bright and early Sunday and then
went with the McGuires to visit friends of theirs about 80 miles
away at a place called Carl Pleasant Lake. We stayed there the day,
boating and fishing. We also had a birthday dinner there in honour
of Bob (one of the boys here) who was twenty one on Sunday.
They had a smashing birthday cake made for him too. We arrived
back at camp deadbeat after a really enjoyable weekend.

Lionel was now entering a different phase of his flying training. By the
beginning of April, his total flying hours had risen to sixty-seven, forty
of which had been solo and seven at night. He still had about three or
four weeks of training left on the Stearman to achieve his 'fixed' ninety-
one hours of tuition before moving on to the more advanced Vultee.
Cross-country flying was also now de rigueur, setting the pilots loose to
navigate from point A to point B and to try not to get themselves lost,
which invariably many of them did. More than one pilot had to come
down on a road by the side of a remote farmstead to ask for directions!

Mr Mills was also still full of surprises, putting on an aerobatic display
to end all aerobatic displays for three of his pupils to see how much they

could take. Two out of the three gave in to their nausea; Lionel managed to keep the contents of his breakfast in his stomach – the benefit, he believed, to taking a weekly dose of senna pods, giving his insides a wall like iron.

With the spring came changes. Squadron Leader Bill Holloway, the OC 4 BFTS, was posted, his place being taken by Wing Commander John McKenna, who had been recognised with an Air Force Cross (AFC) as an instructor in the UK. McKenna was every inch the regular air force officer, and much older than those in his charge. Indeed, he had joined the RAF on a short service commission in 1928!

A further change came with the weather. Cadets were issued with new uniforms in preparation for the near tropical conditions that were heading their way – temperatures in excess of 120 degrees in the shade being the norm. Sunburn had now replaced frostbite as the biggest enemy in failing to adequately cover up.

With spring also came tragedy. Leading Aircraftman Frank Glew, a twenty-year-old lad from Belper in Derbyshire, was on a training flight with his instructor, Barney Gordon, when the aircraft crashed at Red Rock, killing both men. Glew was part of Course 7. Two weeks later, two pilots from Course 5 were killed when their AT6A crashed during a night-flying exercise. LACs Jack Payne and thirty-year-old Ted Hartley were only two weeks away from graduating. It was a terrible month for the students and a sobering reminder of the dangers of flying.

While Lionel may have worried for his own safety, he was far more concerned about his parents in England, and fretted each time that he read about a new bombing raid on London. The Blitz had been over for some time, and the real battles for air superiority were now being fought between the RAF and the Luftwaffe over France and Germany, but every so often a German bomber would get through and the locals would be reminded of the destruction they could cause.

His mother would similarly worry about the dangers of flying and of failure, and Lionel was at pains to reassure her of his safety. He never once mentions the death of his fellow students in any of his letters. A bigger threat than flying, he told her, were the rattlesnakes, and in answer to her questioning as to whether he could retrain as an observer if things did not work out as planned, was that the thought of failure was simply not an option. Lionel was probably in even more danger of falling victim to a jealous girlfriend, for his love interest had moved on from Elaine Nover to Mary Allen Collins, and he jokingly complained that Phoenix was full of pretty girls!

On 15 April he clambered into the Stearman with Mr Mills for his final check and passed:

> That means that I have been recommended for further training on Basic. I feel pretty pleased with myself for having got so far on this course and I can assure you, I am putting in everything I've got to get those wings.
>
> I went up for an expensive solo this afternoon. I was doing quite a bit of inverted flying, when my cigarette lighter and 60 cents dropped out of my pocket. Every time I turn upside down, I lose something. Last week I lost an Indian Silver Tiepin which I bought for $1.50 a couple of weeks ago. It's a good job I was not holding it when it dropped out.

He also found out that his celebrity at being the only Jewish trainee pilot at Falcon Field was about to be usurped. Unusually, he revelled in somebody else's misfortune:

> I have just found out that I am not the only 'Flying Yid' at Falcon Field. There is another chap who has been here about a month. I have not had much to do with him, as I don't like him. He will be going back to Canada shortly, as he crashed a 'plane on the field yesterday. He doesn't look the type of bloke to make a pilot anyway. I should imagine a butcher shop would suit him better. Yesterday afternoon he made his first solo flight. On coming in to land, he levelled out about 50 feet in the air – turned over on his back and crashed to the ground, inverted. He must have been praying pretty hard lately as he wasn't even scratched.

Lionel had better luck with a chance meeting soon after:

Now Dad, here is some news for you. I've always said that wherever you go, you are bound to meet someone you know. Well I guess I must be your Ambassador or something. I spend a month travelling across the Atlantic, over Canada and half way across America and blow me down if I don't meet one of your pals.

Saturday a woman at the British War Relief Society asked me where I came from. When I said Neasden, a gleam came in her eyes. She comes from Hendon. Then I asked her if she knew Joseph Abrahams. She said: 'Is he a little man?' Boy oh boy, that did it. She is Mrs Garner of Hendon. You used to visit her brother and play the piano. She told me to mention Mr A. Woolfson at 15 Ditton Court Road, Westcliffe and Miriam Woolfson at 'Stoep', Ditton Court Road. Her husband's business address is 10 Main Street, Hackney.

You can't imagine how pleased I am to be able to meet someone who knows the family. I mentioned such names as Jeffs – Loudoun – Epitomes – Berudeuis, etc. and she knows them all. However, I haven't been able to spend much time with her yet, but I can assure you that at the earliest moment, I will see her and have a good talk and some Kosher grub. I'll let you know of all developments.

Miriam Woolfson had moved to America in August 1940 with her two children, one of whom had bad asthma. It was thought the cleaner, dryer air would help. She moved first to California and then to Arizona, where she praised the wonderful climate and the sun that shone every day. The Woolfsons were one of several British families who did their bit to make the RAF boys as happy and comfortable as they could, often with planned excursions and picnics.

Events were now moving swiftly for the young Lionel Anderson. Happily he passed his mid-term exams, and his success entitled him to a week's leave. He needed no second bidding, and along with three of his best pals, including Peter Alexandra, began packing provisions for a great adventure: to hitchhike the 400 miles to Los Angeles!

The four boys were lucky, completing their journey in a little over fourteen hours, arriving at 1.30 in the morning, having taken six lifts. They put themselves up for the night in one of the finest hotels, the Baltimore, at a cost of $5 per night. Later that morning, suitably refreshed and catching a few hours' sleep, Lionel phoned his newly acquired family friend, Mr Woolfson, who drove over to pick them up. They spent the day cruising around the local area, taking in the sights of Hollywood, Beverly Hills, Santa Monica, Venice, etc until Mr Woolfson dropped them at the British American Club in Hollywood Boulevard, where they camped out for the rest of the week.

On Monday morning, after breakfast, they decided to pay their old friend Preston Foster a visit at the film studios:

Four of us took a bus out to 20th Century Fox Films Studios in Beverly Hills but were stopped at the gate by a cop who thought we were extras applying for jobs. However, we assured him that we were in the RAF and asked to see Preston Foster. (What a nerve.) Of course we know him as he has been to Falcon Field several times to make the film *Thunderbird*.

He phoned through and much to our surprise we were let in. We were driven over to his set and met the Director of *Thunderbird* Bill Wellman. It was lunchtime then, so we went over to the cafeteria with Preston Foster and Reginald Denny and had dinner. They really made us welcome.

They were all pretty busy finishing this film off, so they got hold of someone with influence to show us around the studios. We were really amazed at the way scenes are faked. There were marvellous replicas of an Hawaiian Island, a bombed London street, Wild West Town, Indian Village and dozens of other things like that. I really can't write down everything I saw. The Fox's lot is simply terrific. It is a town in itself.

We watched Sonja Henie making some scenes for a film called 'Iceland', and met her along with Judy Garland and several lesser known actors and actresses. We had a marvellous time.

Judy Garland needs little or no introduction, having once been described as 'the greatest entertainer that ever lived' by no less a man than Fred Astaire. She was a tiny person (shorter than 5ft), but a massive star, having achieved global stardom for her role as Dorothy in *The Wizard of Oz*. Her private life, however, was nothing short of a disaster, and she was still only twenty.

Sonja Henie was less well known in cinematic terms, but an international star in her own right as an ice skater. Indeed, she was a three-times Olympic champion for Norway before surrendering her amateur status to become a professional performer. Snapped up by Hollywood she was signed to 20th Century Fox, who made her one of the highest-paid actresses of her generation. Not surprisingly, her films tended to maximise her skating prowess.

From the studios, the boys jumped on a bus to the coastal town of Santa Monica, where they had tea and played on the dodgems. In conversation with the locals, who were somewhat amused by the boys' boisterous antics, they learned that Long Beach was only 30 miles away and so once again took to the road. Arriving at Long Beach they had a good look around until in the small hours of the morning they decided upon the next stage of their epic journey – a road trip to San Diego.

They were in a restaurant at the time and, in Lionel's words, 'all felt a bit mad and reckless' so stood by the side of the road to thumb a lift. The lift was quick in coming but the driver was only going as far as Laguna, some way short of their target. Dropped off in the town, it began to rain and so the boys sought shelter in a local nightspot. Smart in their distinctive uniforms, if a little wet, they drew admiring glances from their fellow revellers, particularly female ones. Indeed, two very striking women came over to talk to them and asked where the boys were from. The taller woman had a most particular accent. It sounded foreign – perhaps even German. Lionel recognised her immediately as the film actress Marlene Dietrich, and the lady with her was another actress, Rosalind Russell.

In some ways, meeting film stars was beginning to lose its thrill, but at a practical level neither Lionel nor any of his friends had to stick their hands in their pockets all night, and the drinks were on the house.

After little or no sleep, they started out again, finally reaching their destination at 6.30 on Tuesday morning. The town was crammed full of men in uniform, mostly sailors and marines, and the boys decided to move on, hitching a lift as far as the Mexican border town of Tijuana, where they stopped to take further photographs to add to Lionel's burgeoning collection. Returning to San Diego, they overnighted at a local Young

Men's Christian Association (YMCA) hostelry before heading back to Hollywood, arriving at around five in the evening. The next day they set about exploring Los Angeles, including a visit to the National Broadcasting Company Radio Studios to see Glen Miller in his Chesterfield cigarette programme.

> On Thursday, we set out for Santa Monica again and also visited a small town called Venice. We went to the pictures again and saw Leslie Howard in Mr V. In the evening we met some Canadian girls. We were walking down Hollywood Boulevard when we heard some girls' shouts. They saw our uniforms and thought we were Canadians. We all went to an Ice Show called 'Icecapades', after which we hit another couple of night spots. We turned in at 6 o'clock in the morning.

A big factor in these adventures was the casual friends they made along the way, and the overwhelming generosity of the American people. Frank de Fiesta was one such acquaintance:

> On Friday, we went out with some bloke named Frank de Fiesta. He took us out into the country to a place called Knotts Barry Farm, where we had a smashing dinner of Southern Fried Chicken. Boy it was good. We visited a replica of an old Western town. In the evening, we searched into Hollywood's Earl Carroll's, which is one of the Clubs that the Stars gather. We saw a smashing floor show there and had our photograph taken. Before we left, Earl Carroll bought us a drink. On Saturday, we were out of bed in time to have lunch and had dinner with some second rate English actor named Cooper.

Earl Carroll, a theatre producer and songwriter of some renown, had a tremendous affinity with the flyboys, having been a pilot himself during the First World War. He also had something of a scandalous reputation, associating himself with a former convicted murderer and throwing a party during Prohibition that involved a naked lady in a bath full of illegal liquor. His theatre on Sunset Boulevard was much in demand.

They started their long journey home later that day, and after walking and hitching for a little over eleven hours the boys eventually made it home, exhausted and spent – quite literally as it happens. The rest of the day was whiled away in sleeping. The eight days on the road with his friends had been the most enjoyable holiday Lionel had ever had:

> Boy was I tired. I really had an enjoyable week. It cost me about $45, but it was worth it.

Lionel's complicated entanglements with girls had taken on a further twist during his absence. While his mother was keen for him to pursue his relationship with the Nover's daughter, Elaine (on one occasion Lionel wished his mother would stop 'harping on' about her), Mary Allen Collins was his first choice. But while he was away, a cuckoo had flown into his nest:

> You mentioned in your letter, Mum, that I don't tell you everything as I used to. Personally, I believe I tell you more (but not everything – Woo! Woo!). Gene Tierney's not bad. You asked if I have dropped Elaine for good. Well, actually, the girl situation out here is getting more and more complicated. Mary got engaged all sudden like while I was on leave. (The trouble is that her fiancé – a 1st Lieutenant in the US Air corps keeps blowing into town.) I got sorta hooked by a girl named Pat and Elaine keeps popping up.
>
> It is very surprising the way the girls go on here. It's nothing for a girl to go out with one fellow in the afternoon and then tell him that she will have to leave him early as she has another date for the evening. They get married very young here as well. For instance, this girl is only 17. They nearly all get married by eighteen. Another thing is that even if a girl is engaged, she still goes out with a couple of dozen other guys anyway. No wonder there are so many divorces over here.
>
> I think I'll take up billiards.

The mention of 'billiards' refers to an earlier letter he wrote to his father, who had recently become addicted to the game, as had his mother:

I am glad to hear that you have taken up the noble sport of billiards Dad. I have not played since I left England, as they don't play it here. They have a similar game called Pool though. Billiards seems to be the craze at home now. I was very surprised to hear that you had taken to Billiards, Dad, but Christ! when I heard you had a finger in it too Mum, I nearly did a spiral dive through my bed.

Meanwhile, Lionel's training continued. He had successfully moved from the primary Stearman to the more powerful Vultee BT13.

You should see the inside of the cockpit of these planes, you would have a fit (I did). Levers, switches, dials, handles and pumps all over the damn place. However, I managed to sort things out and I did fairly well on my solo flight today.

With its Pratt & Whitney 450hp radial engine, the aircraft promised to fly faster and higher than the Stearman, and had more sophisticated controls, including landing flaps and a two-position Hamilton Standard controllable pitch propeller. Its modern design, however, did not run to retractable undercarriage, nor a hydraulic system, but was a considerable advance over a biplane.

He had also started night flying in earnest, and had more than 125 hours marked in his logbook. All things being equal, and barring any disasters, he was expecting to have gained his 'wings' by August – more than seven months since he had arrived in the US:

Last Saturday, I went with a load of boys and girls from the British War Relief to a Scouts Cuebio in the mountains about 25 miles out of Phoenix. This Cuebio consists of a swimming pool and a grub house and an open air dance floor. We swam and sun-bathed through the heat of the afternoon and danced in the cool of the evening. Oh boy, it was lovely.

Sunday, I went to the pictures with one of the boys and a couple of girls. We saw 'Andy Hardy's Courtship'. If you want to see a grand film, I advise you to see it. It contains quite a bit of the American slang which I am learning quickly.

I had a very unusual experience last Friday night. Seven of us were asked to be guests of honour at the annual Boy Scouts 'Round Up' in Phoenix. Of course we never refuse invitations and we went. The Kids were informed over the loud speakers that seven British Aviators were in their midst. We were surrounded by scouts demanding our autographs, etc. One of our boys had to say a few words over the mike. Then they had some Red Indians in full war paint and feathers doing their war dance round a fire. We were asked if we would like to enter the sacred circle and be blessed by the Chieftain. Of course we were out for a bit of fun and decided to do it. We were led into this circle by these redskins and stood there while they did a mad dance round us. (I didn't quite like the spears and bows and arrows they carry.) They poured some grain and some-thing over us, which is supposed to be quite an honour, although it itches a bit when it gets down your neck, so I have been paid a com-pliment by a Red Indian Chieftain. (Of course if he was a beautiful blonde I would have liked it better.)

Tonight, I start night flying. I have already done it in the Primary stage of the game, but now we do it in these new basic aircraft. As a matter of fact, I am writing this letter whilst awaiting my turn to go up. It is almost time now, so I will hang on awhile and continue this letter tomorrow.

Lionel's anxiety for his parents' safety increased as news reached the men of a renewed effort by the German Luftwaffe to attack London, in what was seen as a mini 'Blitz'. Friends from home were also steadily enlisting, with many, it would appear, looking to join the RAF. In one letter, Lionel gives a tiny insight into both his love of flying, and his plans for the future. The thought that he could be killed, either in an accident or through enemy action, had not entered his mind:

Stella has told me in her letter that Ronnie is again trying to get in as a pilot. I certainly advise him to try hard, because I know he will like it if he gets through. Not only is it a marvellous experience to travel in foreign lands, but flying itself is marvellous. Before the war, I had no ambitions and no career in front of me. However, since I've been here, I have definitely decided that flying is to be my future peace-time career, either civil or military. Blimey, I never thought I would pass the first Maths exam at Regent's Park. I must admit however, that luck has been with me all the way (touch wood).

In the first weekend in June, a party of thirty of the British flyers clubbed together to hire a bus to take them the 300 miles or so through the desert and across mountain roads to the Grand Canyon. The scenery along the way was breathtaking, and as they neared the Canyon, the desert changed from a scorched landscape of cactus, shrubs and mountains to plains, pinewoods and hills. Lionel had been flying that evening and waited up until three o'clock in the morning to join the party:

> Some of the mountain roads had the side of the mountain on one side and a sheer drop on the other from anything from 200 to 2,000 feet. At some parts it was just like flying. Looking out of the window you could see miles and miles of plain desert about 2,000ft below us, stretching out for miles and miles.
>
> Eventually we arrived at the Canyon 2 o'clock Saturday afternoon. It was really a marvellous sight. A great big hole in the ground, one mile deep and seventeen miles across. The different rock formations are marvellous and the colours are very impressive.
>
> I am afraid my descriptive powers are not great enough to describe this bloody great hole. You just stand there and look at this great big chasm, surrounded by colourful rock formations and the Colorado river running one mile below you. It is so far down that it just looks like a piece of thin silver string.

They stayed overnight at the Bright Angel Hotel, situated in the rim of the Canyon, and returned home the following day, arriving late in the evening.

By the middle of June, Lionel was coming to the end of his training on the basic aircraft. Two more hours of solo flying and he would be due another six days' leave. The 'test' required him to fly a cross-country in three 'legs': the first was flown with a skeleton map; the second flown 'blind' under the hood; and the third was to fly back from wherever he had ended up!

He wondered whether his money would last. To put his wages into context, his 'fortnightly quota', as he called it, amounted to $21. He had blown the equivalent of four weeks' pay on his road trip to San Diego and his wallet was running on empty. As such, he was not making any plans. That is not to say that others were not making plans on his behalf. He was shortly to progress to the advanced trainer, a fast mono-plane that was not too dissimilar to the aircraft he might expect to fly in combat – at least the transition would not be that high a leap. Afterwards he faced a long journey home, via Moncton:

You asked what happens when we finish here. Well, first of all we do six weeks (54 hours) flying on the advanced trainers until August 10th. Then we take our wings examination.

If I pass, and I think I will, I will be sent back to Moncton, Canada, where we will wait another hell-ship. We may be stationed there for quite a few weeks. Some of us will be offered Commissions and stay here as instructors. However, I will turn that job down and do my best to return home and get into the thick of things. We will eventually board a ship and once again be sick and maybe arrive back in good old Angleterre.

We will then be posted to Bournemouth for a week where we will be re-equipped with new uniforms and equipment, etc. and then three weeks leave, during which I will probably be very, very busy. After leave, we go back to Bournemouth and then from there to an Army Unit for a fortnight. Then to a Navy unit for another fortnight. After these few weeks in the Army and Navy (which is to give us an idea of these organisations, etc.) we will be sent to an Advanced Flying Unit (AFU) for a few weeks and then about a month or so at an Operational Training Unit (OTU), where we get used to flying service type aircraft. So now you have got some idea what a British Pilot has to go through before he goes into action.

That was all in the future. In the immediate present, Lionel had many hours of hard study ahead of him to earn his wings, so having successfully completed his basic course, he resolved to take things steady:

> I was very undecided as to what I should do for my leave this time.
> As you know, last time I went to Hollywood, which turned out to
> be very strenuous and also cost me over 40 dollars. Well, this time
> I decided to take it easy, because the last part of our course calls for
> a lot of study and a lot of flying, and last time it took me about a
> week to recover from my vacation. The other reason is that I
> haven't got 40 dollars. However, one of my pals and myself met a
> couple of Mesa girls. The girls are quite nice (but you should see
> their cars), so we decided to stay at camp and go out every day with
> the cars … I mean the girls!
>
> We have just returned from one of the lakes around here, about
> 60 miles away. The girls brought a load of grub and we knew some
> people who owned some boats on this lake (Lake Pleasant), so we
> had a picnic. Not very strenuous (we let the girls row). It was also
> pretty inexpensive. Tomorrow and Friday we shall probably go for
> some long drives, maybe to Canyon Lake (in the mountains) or the
> town of Tucson.
>
> Anyway, will go for a drive somewhere. Next Saturday, Bob and
> myself are going to the small mountain mining town of Globe for
> the weekend. The invitation was extended by a doctor we know.
> He owns his own plane and is going to pick us up at a nearby airport
> and fly us there.

The excursion to Globe was a success, Lionel finding himself fully
absorbed into the beautiful countryside. On his return he dropped into
the British War Relief Society and was introduced to another Jewish boy,
and another aspiring pilot, Leslie Israel. Leslie was a good-looking, sen-
sitive boy who had been privately educated at Haberdashers and later
studied at the Hornsey Art School. He had been a commercial artist prior
to the outbreak of war, and although he loved flying, he hoped to
return to his art when it was all over.

Meantime, Lionel was becoming obsessed with the weather:

> The weather here is really marvellous. Although the tempera-

ture is around 113 degrees and is so gosh darned hot, it isn't too bad.
Our billets are air-cooled down to about 75 degrees. I guess we must
be getting used to the heat.

The heat, however, was indeed becoming a problem. To commence his
training on the new advanced type of aircraft, the North American AT6A
'Harvard', they were obliged to fly at six o'clock in the morning, while
the heat was still bearable. Lionel had precisely 145½ flying hours to his
credit – meaning that he had to acquire a further 54½ hours to complete
the course, hopefully within six weeks. He also had a new instructor.
Mr Mills had executed his duties admirably, but now it fell to his senior
colleague, Mr Ward Miller (who used the call sign when in the air of
Eagle 20), to complete the transition.

> Our daily routine has changed quite a bit since last week. Reveille –
> 04.30. Breakfast 05.00 – Start flying 06.00. Stop flying 10.30 –
> Lunch 10.30–11.15. Ground school 11.30–14.30. Physical Training
> 17.30–18.30. Tea 16.30 and the rest of the time is our own. I am not
> too keen on getting up that time of the morning.

Unfortunately Lionel got off to a false start. Mesa experienced another
one of its dust storms, an incredible phenomenon that instantly negated
all hopes of flying. Flight mechanics and ground staff raced around like
ants whose nest was being attacked, dragging aircraft into hangars if they
could and tying down aircraft to the ground if they couldn't. All of this
was achieved in some of the most terrible conditions, where the men
could quite literally be blinded by sand.

At last the sand storm abated, and normal routines were re-established.
The advanced flying course began, Lionel revelling in the opportunity
to fly the Harvard, that was a step up again from the Vultee and packed
with power. Its Pratt & Whitney Wasp powerplant delivered a top speed
in excess of 180mph, and she could reach a ceiling of more than 22,000ft
if pushed to do so. It also gave Lionel a few more 'gadgets' to think about.

In the first week of July, the heat became intense. The men would cool
down in their own pool that had been built – courtesy of 20th Century
Fox – in gratitude for the RAF's help with the *Thunder Birds* movie:

The heat here is really terrific now. It is usually around 125 degrees during the day. At night, the temperature drops to about 80 or 90 degrees, so you see it gets quite warm. I live in the showers and swimming pool now. I have a cold shower when I get up in the morning, one after dinner, another one after ground school and before tea. After tea I have a dip in our new swimming pool, and before I start night flying I take another shower. Life's just one damned shower after another!

Lionel in deep conversation with his instructor after a training flight.

Chapter 4

Wings

Lionel was studying hard. He had been in America since January and it was now July. He had but a few short weeks to go until his final Wings exam, after which his future would be decided. It was a nerve-wracking time for him and all of the boys; failure could not be contemplated.

Everyone (including me) is studying their notes in preparation for the Wings Examinations which are being held in either two or three weeks, so keep your fingers crossed. With a bit of luck (and a look over the next bloke's shoulder) I should make it. If I don't, I shall want to know why. (And they'll probably tell me.)

Even while he was studying, Lionel was also thinking about the partying that would happen afterwards. A 'tradition' was fast becoming established at Mesa that the success of each course should be celebrated in style, and Lionel was determined not to miss out:

I have just forked out $4 for our graduation dance. We are all looking forward to that. Each Graduating Class has a slap-up dinner and dance at the Hotel Westward Ho! which is the best hotel in Phoenix. We invite our instructors and friends we have made during our stay here and of course we have plenty of girls. The only thing I regret is that you will not be there. However, you can bet that however tight I get, I'll be thinking of you.

Before he could think about getting 'tight', Lionel had to complete two further check flights and the all-important written exams. A requirement of the training programme was also the need to fly in formation with other aircraft, and one such trip took place on 13 July, causing some animation:

> We had a bit of excitement today. We went on a 300-mile cross country flight (solo). Every ship returned except one of the boys. Several of the instructors took off on a search and eventually spotted his aeroplane on the ground. He had run out of gas and made a forced landing on an auxiliary field. He is back now and is as pleased as punch.

With the formation flight completed, Lionel's total hours had risen to 170; he now had only 30 to go and one more flight check before the classroom tests. The exams were to be divided across two different days: Saturday 25 July and Monday 27 July. After that he would know his fate. A funny thing happened on one of their last classroom lectures on armaments:

> During our assessments lecture today, our armaments instructor, a sergeant, discovered some cobwebs on his finger. On investigation, he found a black widow spider on the seat of his chair (which reminds me of an RAF song). He was really lucky as there is no cure for a bite from one of these. Boy, you should have seen airmen run when that thing started to run along the floor; snakes had nothing on that.

At last the first day of the Wings exams arrived, and Lionel headed into the examination room with the abject fear that befalls most students before an important test they know might shape their lives. Only now would he find out whether all of that last minute 'swatting' had been enough. He was far from confident of the result:

> I don't mind telling you that I am not too confident about the results. Most of my papers are OK, but I made a mess of my signals papers. However, if the officers in Washington are very generous, I'll be a Sergeant-Pilot by next Friday. If I do have my Wings up by then, you will receive a Cablegram before you receive this letter.

Lionel need not have worried; the officers in Washington had indeed been generous, not only to Lionel but the entire course; all the same, they experienced an anxious wait to receive their results. They also faced the dreaded interview process. In the US Air Force, all newly qualified pilots were immediately granted a commissioned rank (second lieutenant). This was not the case in the RAF.

A tremendous snobbery existed in the RAF and indeed throughout the Services before the war, regarding the officer corps, and social class was everything. Former public school boys (Old Etonians, Harrovians, Haileyburians, Paulines, Stoics etc) were almost guaranteed to impress the interview board and leave as pilot officers (on probation); so too those with a degree from the right type of university. (Later in the war, the Services could not afford to be quite so choosy.) Whatever the official/unofficial process, Lionel makes no mention of such an interview in his letters, but neither did he seem especially bothered. He was simply thrilled to have passed:

> Well folks, the great day has come. After 28 weeks of intense flying training, I have been given a pair of sergeant's stripes and a pair of Wings. Yes, my dream has come true. I am now a Sergeant Pilot – Boy, am I happy. Tonight, we hold our Graduation dance at the Westward Ho! Hotel in Phoenix and I guess, we'll all make merry.
>
> The last week has been one of great anxiety for my classmates and myself. You see our exam was the stiffest one which has yet been held at Falcon and the results did not come through from Washington until today (four days late). However, when the news came through this morning, there were many whoopees, as we all passed.

This was not actually the case. A number of the pilots found themselves 'reassigned', in US parlance (remustered in RAF terminology). At least one became a navigator, another an air bomber, and one was assigned to the 'Y' Service, listening in on enemy broadcasts.

It was a proud day, however, when Lionel and the majority of boys in his class received their coveted silver wings on parade from their commanding officer. It was a notable and immensely satisfying day also for his US flight commanders – Theodore Hanna (call sign Eagle 19 and later promoted to Assistant Director of Training) and Grayson McFadden (Eagle 34) – and perhaps even more so for his instructors, Messrs Mills and Miller, who had seen all of their young eagles fledge.

Bob Barter, Peter Alexandra and Geoff Bullen, three of Lionel's closest friends had passed, as had John Causton, another pal. Of these four, Peter, Geoff and John were all commissioned.

The parade was the smartest they had ever attended, and the barracks made spick and span for the occasion. Much of the afternoon was spent sewing their new insignia on to their uniforms, such that Lionel's once tidy bedroom now resembled a tailor's shop.

Conversation between the friends now turned to what they would do next. They contemplated the question over an ice-cold beer at a local bar. All pilots started their training on single-engined aircraft and almost all, with very few exceptions, imagined themselves afterwards as fighter pilots, emulating their heroes of the First World War and the current conflict that had seen the rise of the 'ace'.

Of course not all would be destined to fly Spitfires in combat against the best that the Luftwaffe could offer. Some would go on to be trained on twin-engined and subsequently multi-engined aircraft, and find themselves flying bombers over Germany, or long-range patrols for Coastal Command. Some, like Geoff Bullen, who had the appropriate levels of flying skills and attitude, would be retained by the RAF as instructors.

Joe and Debbie Anderson seemed keen that their son should see out the war in what they no doubt perceived as relative safety, teaching others to fly, away from the dangers of flak and bullets. They articulated this view in one of their letters. Lionel, however, had other ideas. His only thought was an opportunity to get to grips with the enemy and shorten the war:

You both seem to like the idea of me being made an instructor and stay out here. Well, here are a few reasons why I am not too keen on the job: 1. I have been away from home about nine months now and I'd like to see what the Old Country looks like. 2. An instructor's job is pretty boring, so it means doing the same thing over and over again, besides taking an instructor's course. 3. There are a load of Jerries to be exterminated. Anyway, they only use the best pilots for that and I am by no means amongst the best.

Lionel is, perhaps, a little unkind in his assessment. He also ignores the
very real dangers that instructors faced in teaching novice pilots, even
in the benign conditions of the Arizona desert. But he is right that the
RAF had a habit of holding on to the best, wherever they could. 'Average'
pilots were expendable, to a greater or lesser degree. 'Above average' or
'exceptional' pilots should not be squandered.

By 1942, all RAF personnel who qualified as aircrew (those who were
not commissioned) were given the rank of sergeant upon obtaining their
'brevet' – whether pilot, observer or wireless operator/air gunner, or
the other 'trades' that would follow in due course as the observer's role
was divided and aircraft became more complicated to handle. Regular
airmen on the ground, who had perhaps put in a dozen or so years of
service to reach the rank of corporal, were understandably resentful of
the practice, although the wisest kept their counsel. Lionel and his contemporaries had effectively 'jumped' three or sometimes more ranks at
a single stroke.

They were, nonetheless, delighted with their new-found status, and
in precisely the right frame of mind to make merry. The graduation
dinner and dance at the Westward Ho! proved a smashing success, and
a small posse proceeded afterwards to a nightclub known as the Grand
to continue the party. By the small hours of the morning, those who were
left continued drinking and eating hamburgers at an all-night diner,
finally making it into bed at about four o'clock in the morning. The
next day, a bleary-eyed Sergeant Lionel Anderson stared into the camera
for the official course photograph (Course 7) and final lecture from their
commanding officer.

The boys were eager to get home, and the authorities equally keen that
they should make room for the next course of trainees. Packing began
in earnest:

This morning has been spent packing my belongings and I am in a
devil of a mess. Some of the boys have been finding all sorts of
queer insects in clothing which has been packed away. One of the

boys found a nest of black widow spiders in his greatcoat (and they're killers). Another fellow found four baby mice in an old kit bag.

They had been told to be ready to depart on 9 August, but not everyone was going back to 'Blighty'. Geoff Bullen, for one, was staying:

> Some of the boys have been recommended as instructors and will only be going as far as Toronto. They are staying in the States too. Jeff Bullen [sic] is one of them. I am sorry to have to leave him as we were good pals all through our training; but I guess that's service life all over; you make friends, really good friends and then you leave them.
>
> We will all be leaving here with mixed feelings on Sunday. I know I shall be sorry to leave this country and all the many friends I have made here; but I shall also be very glad to be on my way home. I sent a cablegram yesterday to tell you of the good news, but it was returned to me by the censor, so I guess you'll have to wait for the air-mail to deliver this letter.

With their packing completed and their farewells said, those personnel of Course 7 returning to the UK started their long journey home first thing on Sunday morning, boarding the California Express at Mesa. The train ride took four days, steaming through a vast expanse of noth-ingness and only occasionally passing a ramshackle collection of huts that had been given an obscure place name. They journeyed through New Mexico, Kansas City and Chicago, stopping over at the 'Windy City' to change trains.

They reached their Canadian destination of Moncton the following Friday, after a further stop in Montreal that enabled Lionel to catch up with some family friends, the Youngs and the Shines, who showed him some of the city. They wrote to tell Joe and Debbie that their boy was safe, and looking taller and healthier than they could ever remember. At Moncton Lionel met up with more friends, and was delighted to see them. After the colour and excitement of Mesa, Moncton seemed positively drab and colourless by comparison, in stark contrast to how he had found the town when he had first travelled through nine months earlier:

Well folks, once more I am on British soil. We left Falcon last Sunday morning and arrived here in Moncton early yesterday morning. I had 3 hours in Montreal and made very good use of them. I called on the Youngs and Judy Shine showed me a bit of the city. I guess you will be pleased to hear that.

Shortly after I arrived in camp, a corporal asked me to report to Wing Headquarters immediately. I wondered what I had done. When I asked him what I was wanted for he said he didn't know, but Pilot Officer (Philip) Braham wanted me; of course I went round there in double-quick time and promptly received an invitation for dinner. He and Ray Braham and their two kids live in a nice apartment near the camp. They were glad to see me and I was glad to see them. As a matter of fact, I am more than pleased.

The last time I was here, I had just arrived from the black-outs and food shortage etc. of England. Also I had only just disembarked from the ship; so you can imagine how marvellous Moncton looked then, with its snow, lights and good food; but this time I have been spoiled by the luxuries I have been enjoying in the States and Moncton didn't look so lovely. There is absolutely nothing to do here and the town (what there is of it) is absolutely lousy with RAF. The grub on the camp stinks. I've only been here one day and I am browned off with it already. However, I won't be here long and will probably be home sooner than you expect.

The letter was dated 14 August. The next day Lionel slipped into the telegraph office to send his parents the cablegram he had been prevented from dispatching at Mesa. This time he was mindful of the censor. It read simply: 'Have been promoted. Hope to see you soon. All my love.'

Fortunately for Lionel, his stay in Moncton was comparatively short-lived and he was soon on his way to Halifax to await a ship home. He was posted to 1 'Y' Depot, and stationed in a camp where he assured his father that the staff were doing all they could to make his stay comfortable, by putting on film shows and concerts, and arranging football and cricket matches during the day.

He left Halifax on 1 September, arriving in New York the next day.
Boarding his ship, he set sail for England on 3 September, the third
anniversary of the outbreak of war, reaching British shores on the 9th and
being posted to 3 Personnel Reception Centre (3PRC) in Bournemouth.
He was billeted at Royal Bath Court, from where he wrote to his parents
on the 12th:

> Just a line to let you know that I arrived safely, after a fairly com-
> fortable journey. We had a parade yesterday afternoon and were
> given new billets.
>
> As you know by now, I am once again in good old England and
> boy, am I pleased to be back. As you no doubt guessed, I immedi-
> ately phoned Mrs Rosen. I met Tony yesterday and we spent the day
> with him. I will probably be here about a week before going home
> on leave. We have to be equipped with clothing, flying clothes, etc.
> Fill out loads of forms and also see the pay accounts. I am very
> disappointed in the fact that I will only be given a week's leave.
> Probably, it is because they don't want to hold up the war too long.

Lionel's frustration is understandable. Having been away for so long,
he might have expected a lengthier period of leave. But then pilots were
also in short supply, and the needs of the RAF were immediate. The air
war was in the balance.

Throughout June, RAF Bomber Command had undertaken a series
of '1,000 bomber' raids, showpiece spectaculars from the new
Commander-in-Chief 'Butch' Harris. In August, a young Australian
group captain was promoted and given charge of a new force of Path-
finders – a corps d'élite in the RAF tasked with finding and marking
targets ahead of the main bomber stream. Both were a portent of what
was to come, and signalled the start of a sustained bombing campaign
that would ultimately take the lives of more than 55,000 airmen. The
fighter boys were under pressure too. For the past year they had been
taking the fight to the Germans, trying to tempt the Luftwaffe into the air
with a series of sweeps and small-scale attacks to tease them into battle. But
they were not having it all their own way and casualties were mounting.

Lionel was pleased, at least, to have the company of friends in

Bournemouth, the Rosens, and was especially close to the son, Anthony. They shared a great deal in common beyond their Jewish faith. Tony had lived in and been to school in Willesden, and volunteered for the RAF soon after his eighteenth birthday. He had trained as a wireless operator/ air gunner (usually abbreviated to wop/ag) and was now fully trained aircrew and wore his sergeant's stripes with pride.

The Personnel Reception Centre was yet another of the RAF's special 'holding camps', where airmen were obliged to bide their time waiting for the administrative machine to catch up with them. Royal Bath Court was well provisioned and well managed, Lionel making mention of the quality of the food in the Sergeants' Mess. It was also a novelty to have others (in the way of orderlies) to clear up after him, rather than being the one doing the cleaning. Lionel was fortunate, also, in having friends close by, and spent time with Tony at a local Jewish club and at the synagogue (Schul).

At a practical level there were things to organise. Lionel was required to hand in his tropical kit and draw new stores more appropriate to his current surroundings. He then spent a joyous week being reunited with his parents in Neasden, and showing them the hundreds of photographs he had taken on his travels.

There were photographs of his outward journey, in the snow in Moncton, the huge Board of Trade Building in Chicago, and the sands of the Arizona desert. There were photographs of the airfield at Mesa, the barracks where they slept and the Mess where they ate. There were pictures of Lionel with his instructor, or in front of a series of unfamiliar biplane and monoplane training aircraft that he had flown and soloed in. There were his friends, Peter, Bob, Geoff, Andy and John having the time of their lives in the surrounding hills and mountains, flipping burgers and drinking beer, dancing with Indians or racing midget cars. And perhaps most fascinating of all were the photographs of the movie stars – Preston Foster, Gene Tierney and Reginald Denny – and the moviemakers themselves with their huge cameras and arc lights.

Lionel had described many of the scenes, events and personalities in his letters, but now here they all were, nine months of his life captured in monochrome, as well as a handful of colour prints. And of course there were the parties, the dances and the girls!

Lionel recounted tales of his adventures, the family friends he had seen and the new friends he had made – the McGuires, the Novers, the Jeffs, the Youngs, the Brahams. Mrs Woolfson and Mrs Garner. The hospitality they had received and the food they had eaten – bananas, oranges, pineapples and ice cream sundaes, as well as the steak and fried chicken. Coca-Cola in the canteen or a milkshake, followed by a game of snooker or pool. The pictures he had seen: *On the Shores of Tripoli*; *The Jungle Book*; *Hellzapoppin'*; *Mr V*; and *Dydea*. Band leaders, film directors and nightclub owners – Paul Whiteman, Bill Wellman and Earl Carroll.

He assured them of the importance of the letters he had received, and the cuttings from the local newspaper that gave folks at home a glimpse into his life overseas. He apologised for the lack of parcels, and explained how the authorities had shortened the rules, and lengthened the red tape.

He listened to the latest from his parents: the friends who had volunteered or been called up and who were now in uniform, many in the serge blue of the RAF. He listened to Gerry and his news: his desire to become an architect, and his exams for Willesden Tech; the buildings he had made and the plans he had drawn; the money he was making with his latest scams and schemes; his cooking and his tomato plants; his first aid, and his miserable experiences as an evacuee; his letters to the editor of the *Willesden Chronicle*, following ably in the footsteps of his father; his dog, Mickey.

In turn, Joe, Debbie and Gerry were enthralled by Lionel's stories and amazed at how much he had grown, both physically and in character. He seemed taller, fitter, healthier – bronzed by the heat of the Arizona desert, a hero in his RAF uniform.

But soon, too soon, his leave was over, and he took the train back to the south coast, arriving to find that he had at last been posted:

Just to let you know that I arrived safely after a fairly comfortable journey. We had a parade yesterday afternoon and were given new billets. This morning we were told that my Flight has been posted. I don't know where to yet, but we will probably be moving out either tomorrow or Friday. I called on Mrs Rosen yesterday afternoon and she tells me that Tony will not be back until next Sunday, so I probably will not see him until – well who knows? I went with some of the boys last night and saw Greer Garson in 'Mrs Miniver'. It is really a marvellous film, guaranteed to make you cry (I nearly did) and suggest that you all go to see it.

The next day, Lionel learned where he was being sent:

My kit has already gone and I leave Bournemouth tomorrow morning 09.00 hrs, my destination is 17 Advanced Flying Unit (AFU) – Watton. I don't think that it will do for a postal address, however, as soon as I arrive, I will let you know my address.
I believe it is somewhere in Norfolk.

Watton was indeed in Norfolk, 9 miles from East Dereham, and built by the contractors John Laing & Son to be a permanent RAF base. That meant it had proper buildings in which to sleep, in preference to the dreaded concrete and corrugated-iron Nissen huts. In general terms, however, the buildings were well designed, well constructed, and offered high standards of comfort and modernity.

It meant also that the station had three concrete runways, rather than grass strips, so were less encumbered by the weather. It had huge, permanent hangars, which allowed the ground crews to go about their work with some protection from the elements, and the whole camp was designed to be 'aircrew friendly' – the accommodation being close to the Mess, rather than a bicycle-ride away.

The RAF had dramatically accelerated its airfield building programme in the late 1930s in preparation for a war it believed had to be coming. Work on several well-known stations such as Cranfield, Marham and Waddington began in 1935, with more famous-named added to the list the following year. Watton was one of the last to be started, and was partially completed by 1937 but fully opened in January 1939 under the command of Group Captain Vincent. It originally served as a base for light bomber squadrons, primarily (at different stages) the Bristol Blenheims of 18, 21, 82 and 105 Squadrons. For a brief period, too, the station was home to 90 Squadron, operating the Boeing Fortress 1 – the only RAF squadron to be so equipped with this mark.

From the autumn of 1942, Watton became home to a new unit, a non-operational training unit known as an AFU. An Advanced Flying Unit was a stepping stone between the training that had been undertaken overseas and an Operational Training Unit (OTU), where airmen would form into crews and prepare for their final posting to a front-line squadron.

Although newly qualified pilots had sufficient experience to fly an aeroplane solo, they had done so in the most benign, not to say perfect, conditions. There was a world of difference, however, between the sun-baked plains of the US or the South African veldt and the blacked-out skies of the UK, especially with the wind howling and the rain coming down in stair rods. Navigating home by following a single railway track on a beautiful summer's day might get a pilot out of trouble in the desert, but was of little use to him over Germany. Pilots who found themselves lost on a friendly cross-country or low on fuel could not simply put down and ask for directions, as had happened during Lionel's time in Mesa.

There was also the need, for pilots principally, to increase their flying hours in different aircraft – ones more closely resembling the planes they might fly on operations. For pilots destined for single-engined aircraft – and fulfilling utopian ambitions of joining a fighter squadron – there was the Miles Master. For those singled out for Bomber, Coastal or Transport Command, there were twin-engined types such as the Avro Anson and Airspeed Oxford. But the greatest need was to give them experience of flying in skies that they shared with hundreds of barrage balloons and thousands of British and German aircraft, and where the night skies could be punctured with the probe of a searchlight beam or the crack of an exploding anti-aircraft shell, even if it was from 'friendly fire'.

Lionel arrived at his new station on 3 October:

Well, I'm here in the wilds of Norfolk, after travelling nearly all day. We arrived here last night (Friday) at about 10.30. Immediately we arrived, we were taken to the Sergeant's Mess, where we were given a really good hot dinner.

It is rather a peculiar arrangement here, as we do our ground school at one aerodrome and our flying from another, so we will be

constantly riding between by bus. Our billets are not as good as
I would like them to be. We sleep in nissen huts – each hut holds
ten men. Our beds are quite comfortable, but there are no lockers.
The main trouble is that the 'doings' and washrooms are in another
building, so that we have to go outside whenever we want to wash.

The best part of this camp is the sergeants' mess. The grub is
really good. I'll go so far as to say that except for the luxuries like
grape-fruit juice, etc. the grub is very nearly as good as the stuff
we got in the States. It is a clean and tidy mess. (That doesn't sound
right – but it is.) The cooks are WAAFs and it is served up to us by
WAAF waitresses – Whoopee!!

Lionel's experiences were not untypical of the time. Most of the larger
bases such as Watton had 'satellite' airfields attached to them, frequently
of less 'permanent' construction and often with grass rather than concrete
runways. Lionel was unfortunate in having to spend much of his time
at the satellite field, where the 'luxuries' were few and far between. He
described his new routine, which involved an early start:

Our routine today was Reveille 06.30 (it's bloody cold that time of
the morning). Breakfast 07.15, Board the R.A.F. bus at 07.30 and
arrive at the other aerodrome by 08.00 hrs. Then the Station
Commanding Officer spoke to us, followed by our Advanced Flying
Unit CO giving us a few do's and don'ts and last but not least, the
CGI (Chief Ground Instructor) told us who's boss around here.
The CGI made me Squad Commander, which I am not too pleased
about, as it means a lot of extra work, trouble and worry.

The bus then brought us back and we had dinner, after which we
returned to the other aerodrome again, to pick up our kit, maps,
parachute (we have our own 'chutes' now). Once again we returned
to our aerodrome for tea.

Our camp is actually a load of huts and small buildings, plonked
in the middle of a field about nine miles from the nearest village
which is Watton, and that is about 15–20 miles from Norwich.

The 'load of huts … plonked in the middle of a field' was RAF Bodney,

4½ miles to the west of Watton and lacking many of Watton's creature comforts. Lionel's parents were less bothered about the perils of flying, and more concerned about their boy's stomach:

> As for that idea of yours, re-sending eatables, we receive a ration of two bars of chocolate per week and fruit is plentiful here. We usually pull up in the village of Watton on our way back from the main field and buy a couple of pounds of pears and plums. And as for cakes, we get plenty of pretty good cake here in the mess for tea. You may be surprised, but I very rarely eat sweets at all nowadays. Anyway, you are rationed for sweets yourselves and I wouldn't want to take that from you. Thanks all the same though. So you see, the grub situation here is excellent. I couldn't wish for better food at all.
>
> My camp is at a place called Bodney. Why it is called that I don't know, as there is nothing round here which can be given a name, except a load of fields and woods. They sent a bus load of WAAFs up here last night so that there should be enough girls to go round.

Flying training at the AFU was destined to last between three and four weeks, depending of course on the vagaries of the British weather. The training was intense, the airmen only being given one day's leave per fortnight. They were, however, free every night, and the station ran a bus into town for the princely sum of 1/6d return.

Bodney was equipped with the Miles Master, an advanced trainer that was in many respects comparable to the Harvard, but in many other ways far better. It had been developed from the Miles Kestrel, an impressive private venture that raised quite a few eyebrows when it first flew in 1937. The manufacturer had anticipated the need for a high-speed monoplane trainer, but despite its remarkable performance (a top speed of 295mph) there was little interest from official circles. Only after the Air Ministry had rejected designs from other manufacturers did they look seriously at the Miles, and placed an order for a modified version of the Kestrel to be called the Master.

The Master prototype, powered by a 715hp Kestrel XXX engine, originally flew in 1938, and the first production variant was delivered to the RAF in May 1939. A Master II flew for the first time six months later, powered by an 870hp Bristol Mercury XX radial engine. Both were capable of speeds in excess of 225mph, and had an impressive rate of climb. Lionel was a happy man when he stepped down from his first dual on Sunday 3 October, but was frustrated not to have flown solo earlier:

> I rather like these kites which are Masters and have done two hours dual on them. I should have soloed today, but there was bad visibility so we couldn't fly.

Poor visibility did not prevent all forms of training, however, since there was always ground instruction on the latest equipment and techniques. And there was more besides:

> I had a bit of a shock in ground school today, when we found that we have to take a course in unarmed combat. You know what that is? It's the correct way to kick a bloke's face in or how to break a Hun's neck while he is trying to bite your ear off. It sounds pretty gruesome, but it's good fun though.

Lionel retained his sense of humour throughout:

> About half an hour ago, the 'phone went in the mess and one of the waitresses called for Sergeant Anderson. As I was expecting a call from a WAAF in Watton, I lifted the receiver and said: 'Hello Ann', and a gruff voice at the other end of the line said: 'Ann buggery, this is Flight-Lieutenant Buchanan (Chief Ground Instructor)!' He wanted me to get my Squad to bring their log books in the morning. I put my foot in it that time!
>
> Well folks, I'll close now. So Cheerio for the present. Love Lionel.

Sadly, this is the last letter that Lionel's mother kept from her son, although it seems somehow appropriate that its content concerns one of his favourite subjects, and one that dominates many of his earlier letters: girls. None of the letters survive in their original form. Debbie meticulously reproduced every item of correspondence, from Lionel's arrival at Heaton Park until his final cheery farewell from AFU, in a pair of hard-backed exercise books, along with notable aerograms, cable-grams and newspaper cuttings.

But it is not all that we know about Lionel's flying career. We are aware that he successfully progressed through AFU, and that his next posting was to an Operational Training Unit (OTU). We also know about the squadron to which he was finally sent, and the very secret work that Lionel did. It was work that had a profound effect on the success of the fighter and bomber war, a world of whispered code words and secret technology. The world of the Moonshine and Mandrel boys.

A Defiant of 256 Squadron – This snapshot of a Defiant, the first aircraft Lionel flew in combat, is one of the last in his personal album.

Chapter 5

The Moonshine Boys

An Operational Training Unit was the logical final step in a pilot's progress to war, preparing men for what they could expect once the muck and bullets started to fly in earnest. Many of the instructors were themselves ex-operational pilots, being 'rested' for six months before returning to the front line.

Lionel left Watton at the end of October, excited at the prospect of what was to come. He had received notice of a posting to 59 OTU on the outskirts of the picturesque town of Milfield in Northumberland – a single-seat fighter training unit. Milfield had opened its hangar doors in August 1942, when 59 OTU moved from RAF Crosby to take up residence, along with its eleven Hawker Hurricanes, six Miles Masters and five Fairey Battles. Aircraft also arrived at Milfield's satellite airfield, Brunton, including a large number of Hurricanes that were said to be veterans of the Battle of Britain.

Although the RAF had recognised the importance of giving trainee pilots an experience of operational life ahead of being posted to a squadron, they had paid little more than lip service to the concept before the war. Courses only lasted two or three weeks, and served principally to convert pilots to the aircraft type they would fly in combat. 'Operational' life was something that they would learn 'on the job', along with the additional training they needed, and it could vary in quality from squadron to squadron, flight to flight, man to man. It took until the middle of 1940 before things began to change, and the emphasis given to equipping OTUs with front-line aircraft and providing operationally experienced instructors at airfields in places that gave fledgling pilots a chance of making it through without breaking an aircraft or their own necks. The units were also run along the same lines as an operational squadron, with the appropriate squadron hierarchies.

By the time Lionel arrived, courses had been extended to up to ten weeks, with thirty or so pilots moving through the system every three weeks, weather permitting. The first five or six weeks followed an accepted pattern: each course was broken down into smaller groups of three or four students allocated to each instructor – a pattern that Lionel was familiar with from his time in the US. Having already mastered the advanced trainer, Lionel was at last given the opportunity to fly one of the most famous aircraft of all time, the Hawker Hurricane. The Hurricane was not as fast or as famous as its sleeker, more agile stablemate, the Supermarine Spitfire, but in Lionel's hands it took on a mythical quality. It could fly faster than anything he had flown previously, as much as 100mph quicker, and with a rate of climb that simply took his breath away.

The Hurricanes at the OTU were mostly tired, battle-weary aircraft that were well past their sell-by date, but kept flying in the absence of newer models that were sent direct to the squadrons. It did not matter. To the student pilots it was the pinnacle of their training, and the ground crews worked miracles to keep their charges on the top line. Hurricanes, of course, were single-seat aircraft; there was no dual before going solo. The instructors, therefore, were careful to go through the cockpit layout and controls in minute detail before letting the trainees loose. Pilots were also provided with Pilot's Notes, a booklet of instructions that provided precise information regarding the take-off and landing speeds of their aircraft, its flying characteristics, and the various hydraulic, electrical and pneumatic systems that helped the Hurricane defy the laws of gravity and bring a pilot safely back down to earth.

Lionel felt like he was climbing into the bucket seat of a racing car compared to the aircraft he had flown before, and was no doubt pleased with the uncluttered and logical layout of the cockpit instruments. In front was the familiar main instrument flying panel with its artificial horizon, air speed indicator, turn and bank indicator, direction indicator and altimeter. Also in his direct line of sight were the large dials of the engine speed indicator, undercarriage indicator and fuel gauge, and a medley of switches, buttons and lights including the ignition switches, boost control cut-out, and fuel pressure warning light. To his left were more switches and buttons with additional cocks and levers, including the throttle lever, oxygen supply cock and trimming tabs for both the rudder and elevators. To his right were many of the emergency devices, including the crucial IFF (Identification Friend or Foe) that would distinguish him as a 'friendly' aircraft to others if his identity were to be somehow in doubt.

Lionel set the fuel cock to 'main tanks on', and adjusted the controls so that the throttle was half an inch open, the propeller control was fully forward, the supercharger control was moderate, and the radiator shutter on. Switching on the ignition, he pressed the starter and booster coil pushbuttons and worked the priming pump as rapidly and vigorously as he could while the engine was being turned. As the engine fired into life, he released the starter button, followed by the booster coil push-button, and screwed down the priming pump. He then opened the throttle slowly until the engine speed indicator showed 1,000rpm and the engine was heating. While the engine warmed up, he tested the various engine and installations, the temperatures and pressures, and ran through a checklist to a pneumonic: T – trimming tabs, ensuring the rudder as fully right and the elevator neutral; P – propeller control, fully forward; fuel – main tanks on, auxiliary tank cock or pump off, pressurising cock set to 'atmosphere'; F – flaps, up; supercharger control 'moderate'; radiator shutter 'fully open'. Now he was ready for take-off.

Easing the throttle slowly to the gate, the Hurricane rapidly picked up speed while Lionel used the rudder to counteract any swing. Within moments he was airborne, and he leaned down to raise the under-carriage, aware of a reassuring 'clunk' as the wheels fully retracted into the wings, and retrimmed the aircraft to be nose heavy. With the under-carriage up, the aircraft soon built up speed until it surpassed an indicated air speed (IAS) of 140mph, the speed at which, Lionel had been told, he could begin to climb.

His first solo was simply to get used to the 'feel' of his new aircraft. It was not a time for extreme aerobatics, though the temptation must have been enormous. After a short familiarity flight, Lionel returned to land, again running through a checklist, lowering the undercarriage and flaps, reducing speed to 120mph IAS and locking the cockpit hood 'open' in case of mishaps. Landing approach was made at about 95mph, comfortably above the stalling speed, and he eased the Hurricane back safely on to the ground, touching the brakes and raising the flaps once the speed had reduced, to taxi back to dispersal, his first flight safely negotiated. Milfield had the advantage of being in the very north of the country, a long way distant from the enemy and the threat of enemy intruders; as such, pilots could solo and conduct local area flying in absolute safety. As well as flying, Lionel also got his first taste of air-to-air firing, shooting at an enormous drogue (rather like an oversized windsock) being dragged behind a Fairey Battle. If he scored anything approaching 8% he would have been considered an ace!

With the first half of the course completed, Lionel and his course transferred to the satellite airfield at Brunton where they continued with more local area flying, sector flying and air-to-air firing but this time in flight, and then squadron formations in simulated combat conditions. By now, the pupil pilots were almost fully trained combat airmen, and since they were flying armed aircraft, they became a de facto operational squadron. The students and instructors were even given a squadron designation – 559 Squadron – with the knowledge that if they were on training detail and at flight strength (ie four aircraft), they could be called upon to intercept any hostile intruders in the sector. This was known as the 'saracen scheme', and although the anticipation of enemy action caused much excitement, they never got the chance to put theory into practice.

The weeks passed quickly and a new year dawned: 1943. Perhaps this would be the last year of the war. The Germans were on the run, or rather besieged, in Stalingrad and their surrender imminent – a surrender that would mark a turning point in the war in the East; the once mighty Afrika Korps had been defeated at El Alamein and were retreating in North Africa, and Churchill and Roosevelt, the US President, were already discussing their goal of achieving the Axis nations' unconditional surrender.

In contrast, Lionel had been checked out by the chief flying instructor (CFI) and deemed ready for operational life, his logbook duly signed to attest to his flying ability. The waiting was at last over. Lionel no doubt dreamed of being sent to a front-line Spitfire squadron, or perhaps one

of the squadrons now flying the RAF's very latest fighter and successor
to the Hurricane, the Hawker Typhoon. He had heard much about the
Typhoon; it had been the talk of the OTU, and some of the senior officers had even flown one. Indeed, his OTU would soon after be equipped
with the beast, a moody aircraft with an unfortunate habit of losing its
tail mid-flight. He wondered whether the fates would be kind.

A signal arrived: a posting to 515 Squadron at Heston. He had heard
neither of the squadron, nor of the airfield. But he had heard of the
aircraft he was destined to fly – the Boulton Paul Defiant – and his disappointment could not have been more intense. Lionel was officially
posted to 515 Squadron on 27 January, and greeted by the adjutant who
told him something about the squadron's story. The squadron, he learned,
was comparatively new. Its lineage could be traced back to May the previous year, while Lionel had been studying for his 'Wings' exams in
Arizona, and the Defiant Flight had been formed at RAF Northolt.

The RAF had been prosecuting an offensive air war from the very
beginning. Although many of its early forays into enemy airspace were
little short of disastrous, both during the day and at night, a great many
lessons had been learned, and this knowledge was now being put into
practice. The first incumbents within Bomber Command, for example,
had been replaced, such that by February 1942 it had a new leader, Air
Marshal Arthur Harris, who would lead the force until the end of the
war. Harris believed that aerial bombing at an intense and uncompro-
mising level could win the war, and set about to prove that his theory
had merit. He was astute enough to recognise that his 'boys' needed an
injection of morale. Similarly, he was intelligent enough to know that
he needed to win the public relations battle in order to garner support
from those best placed to provide it, for there were many who doubted
the capabilities of Bomber Command, and were jealous of its resources.
Harris achieved an early victory, with concentrated raids on Lübeck
and Rostock inflicting tangible damage to the enemy's transport system.
Buoyed by this success, Harris created the first of his 'spectaculars', a raid
on Cologne at the end of May involving more than one thousand aircraft. That he had to beg, borrow and virtually steal aircraft from Coastal
Command and various training establishments to reach the magical

number is not the point; it was a tactical and PR triumph, and was followed up soon after by a series of similar raids. Now Harris had the ear of the Prime Minister, and a comparatively free hand (in the immediate period at least) to experiment to the full.

But there was a problem with putting so many bombers in the air at one time: they could be easily tracked by enemy radar. It had not only been the RAF that had been investing in new technology and thinking. For every advance by one side, there was a counter-development from the other. With the increased onslaught from Bomber Command, the Germans had established a defence infrastructure par excellence, with corridors of searchlights and heavy flak batteries ready to meet the incoming wave of aircraft. They had also moved squadrons of night fighters into the attack, guided to their quarry by sophisticated ground and air radar.

Bomber losses began to mount. In February 1942, a total of 1,162 aircraft were dispatched on raids over occupied Europe, resulting in 18 aircraft being lost and a further 64 damaged. In June 1942, when Bomber Command operations were at their peak for the year, out of the 4,801 aircraft that took off, some 199 went missing and a further 442 were damaged, mostly by flak but an alarming number by enemy night fighters. Such losses could not be sustained, and Harris knew that it would get worse before it could get any better.

At the core of the German defences was an early warning radar system called Freya. Named in deference to a Norse goddess, Freya was not a single radar but rather a network of systems installed along the enemy coast. (Freya stations were located at Cap Barfleur, Cap d'Antifer, Cap de la Hague, Channel Islands, Saint-Brieuc, Caen, Dieppe, Gris Nez, Domburg, Le Touquet, Den Hague's-Gravenhage, and La Panne.) It was an integral part of the Kammhuber line ordered by the Luftwaffe chief, Hermann Goering, to counter the first British raids and established by Oberst Josef Kammhuber, after whom the defences were named. Operating on a 1.2m wavelength (250MHz), Freya used only comparatively small antennae (especially compared to Britain's Chain Home radar) and as such was more readily transportable. It also offered a higher resolution, allowing even the smallest targets to be identified.

Freya was capable of detecting an approaching aircraft from a range of up to 100 miles, and as such represented a threat to all RAF operations and not just Bomber Command. Fighter sweeps (search and destroy missions known as 'Rodeos') and escort operations in support of light- and medium-bomber operations over enemy airfields and specific targets (known as 'Circus' or 'Ramrod' operations depending on the particular purpose) also needed to be protected. These fell within the remit of 11 Group, then under the command of Air Vice Marshal Trafford Leigh Mallory. Indeed, Leigh Mallory had written to his immediate superior, Air Marshal Sholto Douglas – the Commander-in-Chief of Fighter Command in April 1942 – about the increasing losses his forces were suffering, with specific mention of the enemy's radar defences: 'His [the Germans'] RDF system has improved so much in the last few months that it is very difficult to get a formation into France without it being detected and reported with great accuracy.'

There were several ways that the potentially devastating impact of Freya could be minimalised. One involved creating a 'spoof', deceiving the German radar into thinking that there were many more aircraft in the sky than were actually present. Another comprised a 'screen', jamming the radar to the extent that a large number of aircraft could pass, effectively 'unseen'.

The challenge was given to the scientific marvels at the Telecommunications Research Establishment (TRE) in Malvern. For the 'spoof', they developed what was known as the Airborne Radio Installation Transmitter Receiver (ARI TR1427 to give it its full technical specification). It worked by receiving pulses from the Freya installations, amplifying them, and sending them back, hence creating the illusion of a much larger force flying in formation. The code name for ARI TR1427 was 'Moonshine'. For the 'screen', the scientists created 'Mandrel', a noise jammer that overwhelmed the signals from Freya. This too was a radio transmitter that, like Moonshine, could be carried in the air.

For Moonshine to work effectively, a small number of aircraft equipped with the device would be obliged to fly in formation in daylight until such time as the spoof prompted a response, at which point they could break formation and fly home independently. The tactic for Mandrel was somewhat different. It required the aircraft carrying this equipment to fly out into the night until they reached a specific patrol area, approximately 50 miles (80km) off the enemy coast. Here they would orbit, sometimes for an hour or more, until such time as the weather, shortage of fuel, or the unwelcome sight of a German fighter, obliged them to return home. By using nine aircraft, each with their designated orbit, a 200-mile (320km) 'screen' could be made in the Germans' radar coverage – a gap big enough to allow a steady stream of bomber aircraft to progress to their target, as yet unseen.

The challenge was in finding out whether the boffins' theories held true in practice. The challenge also was in convincing the High Command where their resources should be best allocated. The first argument was around what kind of unit – and what type of aircraft – were to carry the new equipment. Did it require a whole new squadron to be created, or could a smaller flight be just as effective, but far less costly in men and materiel? And where should the new unit be based? The second argument focused on the devices themselves, and how they might be best deployed. Moonshine and Mandrel were new and untried, and would afford the RAF command a competitive advantage, but only for a limited period. Once the secret was out of the bag, the Germans would be quick to develop a countermeasure, and the advantage would soon be lost. Should both technologies be used simultaneously, or should one be held in reserve, for use at some unspecified time in the future?

The former was resolved only after a full and frank exchange of views by those senior commanders with a vested interest. An initial plan to create a new squadron comprising twelve plus six aircraft operating from RAF Northolt was overruled in favour of creating a smaller 'flight' with an initial strength of nine aircraft commanded by an experienced flight lieutenant with the support of at least two other seasoned officers. The remaining pilots (according to the minute dated 6 June 1942) need not have the same levels of expertise or seniority.

The latter issue similarly prompted fierce debate. Sholto Douglas became a keen advocate of Moonshine: 'I have come to the conclusion', he wrote (in a letter dated 18 May), 'that it would be advisable to employ this device as soon as it is ready for operational use. We are at present engaged in offensive fighter operations against the enemy across the channel, whereas he is on the defensive and rarely approaches our shores except in small numbers. It would be to our advantage to employ Moonshine at the first opportunity.'

Douglas got his way, but in the use of Mandrel he was more circumspect, and took heed of the warning issued to him by Sir Henry Tizard at the Ministry of Aircraft Production who wrote: 'By using Mandrel we shall be teaching him (the enemy) a form of jamming which would be most effective against us, and no countermeasure is likely to be available for a long time.' The C-in-C responded (letter of 13 June 1942) that he would not use Mandrel '… until a big operation comes along that would justify giving it away. I doubt if I shall in fact use it until the spring.'

Moonshine was thus literally and metaphorically cleared for take-off. There was agreement on the new Flight; there was agreement on where that Flight was to be based; and there was accord on the aircraft that would carry the secret equipment: the Boulton Paul Defiant.

The Defiant was considered largely obsolete. It was a somewhat unique aircraft, one of the RAF's very few 'turret' fighters, and had been originally intended as a day fighter. Rather than a bank of forward-firing Browning .303 machine guns in its wings, as per the original Spitfire and Hurricane designs, the Defiant had a machine-gun turret mounted behind the pilot and operated by the second man in the crew, an air gunner. The turret was hydraulically powered with a crank-operated mechanical backup. The guns were electrically fired, and insulated cut-off points in the turret ring prevented the guns from being activated when they were pointing at the propeller disc or the tail.

The concept looked encouraging on paper, and indeed the 'fighter' claimed a number of successes in its first battles over France that preceded the Battle of Britain. But its weaknesses were quickly exposed. Although an impressive design, the weight of the four-gun turret and the additional crew member significantly impacted the aircraft's performance; the turret was also not able to traverse 360 degrees, which rendered the aircraft virtually defenceless when attacked from certain quarters. Losses began to mount, and the aircraft was relegated to a night-fighter role, where it achieved something of a rebirth. By the spring of 1942, however, the Defiant was all but washed out and many were being converted to target towing (TT) duties or similar. A handful, however, were set aside for special operations, and equipped with the new TRE technology.

Test flights were carried out towards the end of May, with regular RAF pilots flying with civilian scientific engineers in the rear turret where the Moonshine equipment was installed, the tests being flown from the secret Aeroplane and Armament Experimental Establishment at Boscombe Down and from Tangmere on the Kent coast. On 20 June, the 'experienced flight lieutenant' arrived to take command of the Flight. His name was Flight Lieutenant Samuel Thomas and he was exactly the kind of seasoned officer they were looking for and had envisaged.

Only days before, Thomas had been awarded the Distinguished Flying Cross (DFC) for a tour of operations with 264 Squadron, one of the first Defiant squadrons that had seen action during the Dunkirk evacuation and subsequently. He came with a small number of confirmed victories to his name, but also the scars of having to bale out, having been at the wrong end of a battle with a gaggle of Messerschmitt Bf109s, and having had the trauma of witnessing the death of his air gunner, LAC John Bromley.

Experimental flights continued throughout June and July as the Flight's strength increased in ones or twos as pilots and air gunners were posted in from various OTUs and other training establishments. Many of the gunners, in particular, were very experienced men who had come through the Battle of Britain and even the Battle of France, and some had been decorated. The gunnery leader (the senior air gunner), Flight Lieutenant Derek Smythe, was unusual in that he had joined the RAF on a direct commission in April 1940, and was remarkable for having fought in France with 98 Squadron and survived, the squadron all but decimated. Re-turning to the UK he was posted to Aston Down to convert from Fairey Battle monoplane bombers to Defiants, and joined 264 Squadron at Duxford at the start of the Battle of Britain. He fought throughout the battle and again survived to be posted to 515 Squadron at the end of June 1942.

Fred Gash was also ex-264 Squadron, having joined the unit in August 1940. He and his regular pilot had formed something of an 'ace' team, shooting down two enemy bombers in daylight and two more at night – a considerable achievement for the time. For their efforts Gash received the Distinguished Flying Medal, and his pilot – Des Hughes – the Distinguished Flying Cross, their awards being gazetted in April 1941. (Hughes went on to become one of the war's most decorated night-fighter

The Anderson family. Debbie, Joe and the two boys before the war. Life was hand to mouth.
(All pictures courtesy of the Anderson Family)

Mother, Debbie Anderson, who never recovered from the death of her firstborn.

Father, Joe Anderson – an inveterate letter writer who clashed with his wife and younger son.

An early self-portrait.

Mary Allen Collins – one of Lionel's many love interests who got herself engaged while he was on leave!

Lionel developed his sense of adventure as a young boy.

ACRC, Regent's Park – Lionel is second row, seated far left. His journey was just beginning.

Gill Jones, Peter Alexandra, Mr Mills (Lionel's instructor), Lionel and John Causton.

Ground loops were among the most frequent accidents.

Lionel grinning from the cockpit of a Vultee.

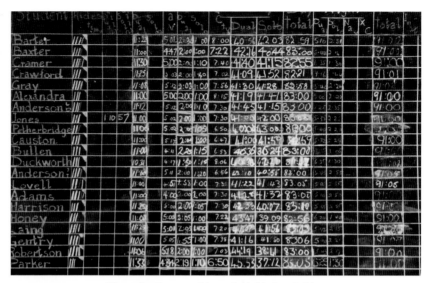

The students' progress is recorded in black and white.

The graduation dance at the Westward Ho! hotel, ended with eating hamburgers at a late-night diner.

The men of Course 7 with their flight commanders Hanna and McFadden at the end of their 91 hours primary.

Tony Rosen (left) with Lionel, both as qualified sergeant aircrew. Both did not survive the war.

Left John Causton and Lionel larking around for the camera at the midget car track.

Below Peter Alexandra, Geoff Bullen and Lionel – three firm friends. Only one would survive the war.

A barbecue with friends in the surrounding mountains.

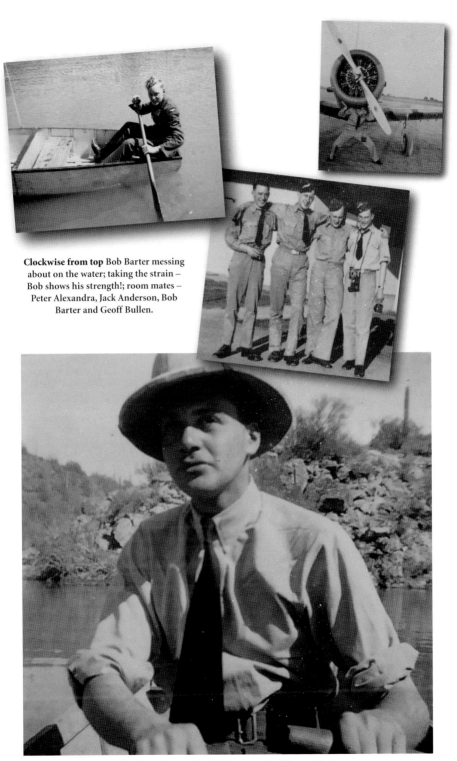

Clockwise from top Bob Barter messing about on the water; taking the strain – Bob shows his strength!; room mates – Peter Alexandra, Jack Anderson, Bob Barter and Geoff Bullen.

Lionel complete with pith helmet on Carl Pleasant Lake.

Above The caption on the back of this photograph reads: confined to barracks!
Above right Bob Barter graduated as a sergeant pilot.

Peter hams it up for the camera on the epic 400-mile hitchhike to Los Angeles.

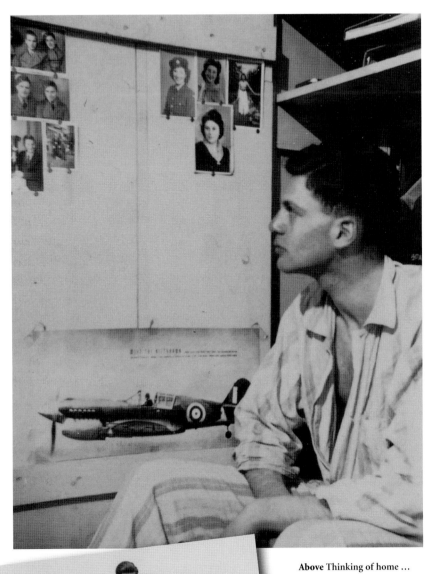

Above Thinking of home …

Left Lionel and Geoff catch up on some reading.

Below Carl Pleasant Lake – from the air; Jack Anderson and Lionel in the South Mountains.

Top and above Native Americans in full war paint at the annual Boy Scouts 'Round Up' in Phoenix.

Lionel made it as far as the Mexican border town of Tijuana before heading for San Diego.

Above Lionel looking unusually glum at the arrival of a visiting Lockheed Hudson aircraft; newly qualified sergeant pilots on the long train journey across the US and Canada.

A formal portrait (printed in February 1942) hanging in a large frame; it may have been the template for similar portraits of the Tracy brothers.

Above Actor Reginald Denny shares a joke with two RAF cadets; Preston Foster arrives on set with his co-star, Gene Tierney.

Camera, lighting and production crews 'on set' for the filming of *Thunder Birds*.

RAF trainee aircrew line up on parade as Hollywood extras!

A bombed London street – Hollywood style.

The actor Jack Holt takes a break between scenes.

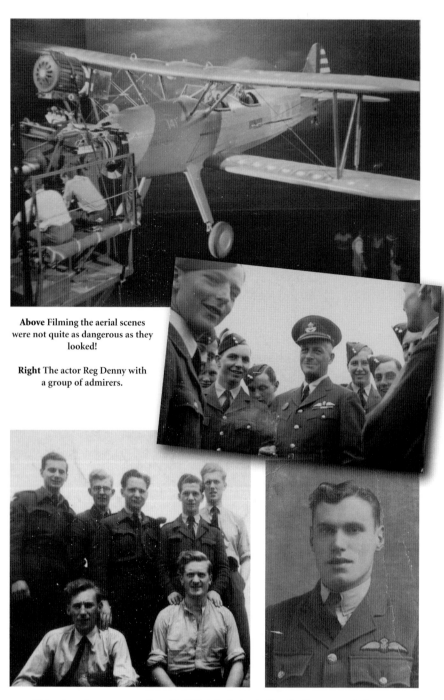

Above Filming the aerial scenes were not quite as dangerous as they looked!

Right The actor Reg Denny with a group of admirers.

Above An unknown group of 'sparkies'. Their inclusion in Lionel's album suggests they are 515 Squadron ground crew. **Above right** Harry Whitmill – the first of the 'old guard' to be lost after converting to Mosquitoes.

pilots, retiring as Air Vice Marshal F.D. Hughes, CB, CBE, DSO, DFC and two bars, AFC.)

Another former 264 air gunner was Oswald Hardy. He had similarly been posted to the squadron in the summer of 1940 and taken part in one of the Defiant's last day-fighting engagements, but had the misfortune of being shot down. Happily he survived, as did his pilot, Jim Bailey. The following year, Hardy was brought down at night by friendly fire and obliged to bale out over London, breaking both legs on landing. Having fully recovered he was commissioned and posted to 515 Squadron.

Eric Ferguson had also taken part in the Battle of Britain, in the later stages, as an air gunner with 141 Squadron at Drem in Scotland. A former sergeant, he had been commissioned as a pilot officer in February 1942. Not all of the gunners were familiar with the Defiant, but that did not mean that they lacked experience. Reg Dunbar was a case in point. Reg had joined the RAF at the tender age of seventeen and a half, and having trained as an air gunner was posted to 37 Squadron, operating the Vickers Wellington. He flew his first operation in May 1940 as a rear gunner, and remained at the back of the aircraft for his first seventeen operations, after which his crew was tour expired and he was obliged to complete his next thirteen operations with a different pilot. Sent on a month's leave, he had been at the railway station awaiting his train home when he was told to report to the station master's office on platform one. He was given a message from the squadron's officer commanding, Wing Commander Merton, requesting that he returned to base. Reg's pilot, a squadron leader, was being posted to the Middle East, and wanted Reg to go with him. He did, completing a second tour and then returning to the UK for a 'rest' at OTU in early 1942.

While 'resting' at Harwell he took part in two of the first 1,000-bomber raids – aircraft from the training units being pressed into service to reach the magical number required for maximum publicity. They drew lots to see which aircraft they would take, Reg being assigned a Pegasus-engined Wellington that reeked of fuel and would not climb above 6,000ft. After this experience, Reg volunteered for Special Duties, believing it would be safer.

The flying schedule was relentless, with aircraft in the sky from dawn to dusk, weather permitting. Perhaps not surprisingly, the exhaustive regime began to take its toll on man and machine alike, resulting inevitably in tragedy on the evening of 8 July.

Five aircraft took off to practise formation flying when one of the Defiants suffered an engine failure. Pilot Officer Cyril Leonard called his flight commander over R/T (radio transmission) to say that he had a problem and would attempt a forced landing at Aldenham, a small airfield not far from their Northolt base. Gliding such a heavy aircraft in to land with no power was a difficult feat, and pilot Leonard misjudged his approach, landing short of the runway. In undershooting, his aircraft struck a tree and cartwheeled, killing him outright. His air gunner, Pilot Officer Simmonds, was badly shaken but otherwise unharmed and was taken to hospital in Barnet. (Leonard was buried five days later at Rose Hill Cemetery in Oxford.)

The first opportunity to use Moonshine operationally eventually came on 6 August, but when one of the nine Defiants suffered engine failure, the flight was abandoned. Later that same day, however, nine aircraft again took off in the early evening and this time completed their operation without incident but with complete success. Orbiting over Portland, it was estimated that they were within range of the enemy radar for about an hour before returning to base. The enemy reacted to this 'intrusion' by raising the balloon barrage at Cherbourg and sending up every fighter available in that sector from its airfield at Maupertus. An operator in the 'Y' service listening in to a German report said later: 'We listened as 30 German 'planes, the entire defence of Cherbourg, took to the air! A short while later, the Moonshine Defiants laid a "spoof" over the Thames that allowed US Flying Fortresses plus fighter escorts to attack Rouen. The Luftwaffe sent 144 planes to intercept the spoof but only a small number to Rouen.'

These first operations were all undertaken in daylight and at great danger to the crews, who had to fly in formation for maximum effect. Each Moonshine transmitter could only cover a part of the Freya radar's frequency, but only eight or nine Defiants were required to give the impression of more than 100 aircraft and sow complete confusion among the enemy defences. Keeping the enemy guessing, or sending them off in the wrong direction, could have a dramatic impact on the success of each raid, but it was done at considerable risk to the crews of the Defiants.

Their tactics were simple: after take-off the aircraft would rendezvous with their escort over a fixed point and climb to a height of around 15,000ft. The fighters would take up position above them. The Defiants would fly to within 35 miles of the coast and then the gunners would switch on their airborne transmitters and wait to see the enemy reaction. As soon as the Germans had taken the bait, the Defiant pilots would turn the aircraft around, dive for the deck and return home at full speed. The escort aircraft would carry out their own duties independently. The purpose at all times was for the 'spoof' force to keep the German fighters away from the 'real' force, regardless of its size.

Throughout August the Flight established a busy routine and nearly lost another aircraft on the afternoon of 12 August when Pilot Officer Wingfield was obliged to crash-land his Defiant at Tangmere, fortunately without injury to himself or his air gunner. (The squadron had been detailed to fly a test flight without its Moonshine equipment switched on to verify that the results of the earlier flights had not been down to luck. It would have been ironic to have lost a pilot on an exercise purely to satisfy the sceptical minds of the 11 Group Air Staff!)

The Flight undertook a most important role on the morning of 19 August. The Russians had been pressing for their Allies to open a second front in the west to ease the pressure on their own forces in the east, and split the German defences. While a full-scale invasion of France was not then practical, a plan was proposed by Combined Operations for a 'raid in strength' on a French coastal town, to destroy certain military installations and to act as a rehearsal for future operations. The operation was code named 'Jubilee', and the French town in question was Dieppe.

The Canadian forces picked for the attack hit the beaches at dusk, but by late morning the operation was already going badly wrong. The RAF was also having a hard time of it, so much so that the day was known as 'the greatest air battle'.

The Defiant Flight's role in Dieppe does not seem to appear in any of the published records, but nine of their aircraft took off at 11.00 hours to create a diversion for a Circus against Abbeville (a well-inhabited German fighter station) in support of the combined operation, and in an attempt to draw the German day-fighter force away from where the action was really taking place. Despite their best efforts, 'the greatest air battle' also proved to be one of the worst days for the RAF, the junior service losing 100 aircraft to enemy action or accidents, with a further 66 aircraft damaged. Some 64 airmen were killed, mostly pilots, and a further 36 were captured, wounded or injured.

After the disappointment of Dieppe, the Flight recorded its most successful operation in its short history on the morning of 21 August when along with three Wings of fighter aircraft it provided a diversion for an actual attack on Rotterdam (Circus 207). More than 100 German fighters were steered towards the 'spoof', allowing the 'real' force a safer run to the target.

On 9 September, Sam Thomas, recently promoted to squadron leader, departed for a well-earned seven days' leave, but that did not mean that the rest of the Flight was excused service. Several daylight Moonshine operations were carried out during his absence. He returned on 19 September, refreshed and awaiting his next challenge – one that came at the end of the month when the Flight was officially elevated to squadron status. Fighter Command HQ had originally wanted to wait, but in the end relented to the reasoning from HQ 11 Group. On 1 October the Defiant Flight formally became 515 Squadron, with the motto 'Strike quickly to kill the enemy'.

The squadron and its new officer commanding did not get off to an auspicious start. On the very first day of its new beginning, Sam Thomas was practising night landings when his brakes failed and the aircraft swung across the flare path and did a complete about turn, at which point the undercarriage collapsed. Fortunately, Thomas and his senior air gunner, Flight Lieutenant Derek Smythe, emerged from the crash unscathed.

Accidents and serviceability were features of everyday life on an operational squadron, especially those men operating aircraft who were already tired. The Defiant seems to have had issues with the strength of its undercarriage, since the majority of minor accidents appear to have a common link. Air leaks, oil leaks, brake pressure failure, oxygen failure and R/T breakdown could all cause an aircraft to be grounded or an operation 'scrubbed'. If such occurrences happened in flight, the more serious could result in the pilot having to make a forced landing, or sometimes even a crash-landing. On 11 October, for example, two Defiants suffered engine trouble, and both pilots were compelled to land away from base. One pilot, finding his windscreen smeared with oil, could not see the runway properly and overshot, damaging the undercarriage. Additional ground staff in the form of electricians, fitters, flight mechanics and maintenance assistants, were drafted in to help keep the aircraft in the air.

On 17 October, the squadron had an establishment visitor in the form of the Right Honourable Sir Archibald Sinclair, the Secretary of State for Air. Escorted by the station commander, the minister took great interest in the squadron's aircraft and its crews and did not leave until late in the afternoon. A further dignitary arrived four days later, this time from the United States Treasury. He was treated to a forty-minute flying display.

Discussions, meanwhile, were well under way as regards the squadron's future. Moves were afoot to disband the unit as being 'wasteful' on men and machines. The official organisation now comprised fourteen pilots, fourteen air gunners, one air observer, and sixteen plus two aircraft, all of which were fitted with Moonshine. In a memo dated 18 October 1942, the Group Captain, RDF (Radio Direction Finding) Plans, defended the role of 515. He explained away the large number of aircraft on the establishment by citing the unreliability of the Defiant: 'It must be remembered', he wrote, 'that at least nine aircraft must be in the air at the same time in order to cover the complete range of frequencies used by Freya.' He added: 'I feel it would be unwise to disband the Squadron after we have gone to some pains to make "Moonshine" a working proposition' and that the Senior Air Staff Officer (SASO) at 11 Group considered Moonshine was 'still in its infancy ... and a valuable tactical weapon in getting the hun off the ground when weather conditions are too bad to justify a full scale offensive operation.' He recommended that 515 Squadron be left to continue its good work.

At the end of the month a signal was received for the squadron to move to a new base, RAF Heston in Middlesex. A forward party proceeded to Heston in the morning of the 29th, followed by the main party two hours later. The aircraft were flown from Northolt to Heston in the afternoon, but again not without incident. Pilot Officer Wingfield was again forced to land at a small airfield called Heath Row, damaging his aircraft in the process. Moving stations required considerable effort, and it is a great testimony to Thomas and his administrative team that the transfer was completed with such speed and efficiency. Within days the squadron was ready for operations again, but this time with the second of the TRE's secret devices that the C-in-C Fighter Command had now given his permission to use.

Moonshine had served its purpose, and been incredibly effective, but the Germans were becoming wise to it. Needs were changing. Mandrel, for so long held in reserve, was now cleared for action. The squadron was to be assigned a new role.

The clues were there for those who chose to look: aircraft came and went; night-flying training intensified in preference to daylight trips; a new special signals officer arrived from 11 Group headquarters; a Mosquito night-fighter crew was attached from 23 Squadron. Operations were still flown, but their frequency declined, which meant fewer accidents. New equipment was installed with a new code name.

For a Mandrel operation the squadron adopted a new tactic. They would leave Heston in the late afternoon for other RAF stations nearer to their ultimate patrol areas: Coltishall on the Norfolk coast; Tangmere in West Sussex; and West Malling in Kent were preferred. Here they would refuel, and take off again in the early evening and be 'controlled' to their designated areas by specialist controllers within Fighter Command. If all went well they would land back at their advanced base around two hours later, at the edge of their endurance, and fly back to Heston the following day. Assuming they were not required for further operations – and assuming they made it back at all.

This is not being dramatic. Once the Defiant crew reached its patrol area, the gunner had to drop down inside the fuselage of the aircraft to operate the Mandrel set, and keep the dial on the correct Freya frequency. While he did so, the Defiant was effectively defenceless; the turret was unmanned, and the ground controller was not able to warn his charge of any incoming enemy fighters for fear of interfering with the jamming operation.

The squadron was ready for its first Mandrel operation on the night of 5/6 December 1942. At just before six in the evening, the CO set off for the twenty-minute hop down to West Malling in the company of his deputy. Two other aircraft set off shortly after for Tangmere. Just prior to their departure a serious accident happened. One of the ground crew, an expert in RDF, was fitting a detonator to the new secret equipment when the detonator exploded in his hand, causing terrible injuries. It was perhaps a portent of the days ahead.

The first operation did indeed appear jinxed. Poor weather meant it was eventually scrubbed, and the four aircraft returned to Heston the following morning. Later that same day another operation was planned, this time involving eight aircraft and fortunately having a little more luck: three set out from West Malling, three for Coltishall and two from Tangmere, all of them returning safely.

This became the pattern over the next few weeks, the squadron consistently putting seven or eight aircraft into the sky on every night that the weather allowed. There was even some excitement courtesy of their 'guests' from 23 Squadron who managed to chalk up a red-letter day – or rather night – in the second week of December, destroying two enemy aircraft in a single night and damaging two more.

Two weeks before Lionel arrived, there was another major incident, again the result of the weather that was proving as much of an enemy as the Germans. Sergeant Thomas Ecclestone was attempting to land at Heston in the most atrocious conditions. Visibility was down to less than 600yd and he was denied the choice of landing elsewhere, due to the fact that 'elsewhere' conditions were just as bad. Easing the heavy Defiant down on to the runway as best he could, he completely failed to see a visiting Wellington bomber and the two aircraft collided. Both aircraft were badly damaged, but happily Ecclestone and his gunner emerged without a scratch.

It was not until almost four weeks after this incident, and the court of inquiry had exonerated Ecclestone of all blame, that Lionel at last had his chance to fly the Defiant. He took Defiant AA582 to Coltishall from where he carried out two practice exercises, familiarising himself with the aircraft, the technique, and having another man in the aeroplane behind him – at least one who wasn't an instructor.

The flight was not an unpleasant experience. For its time, the cockpit of the Defiant was comparatively roomy and well laid out. Something he noticed immediately was the mounting of the control column on an extension of the seat, so that when the seat was raised or lowered, the stick remained in the same relative position. The Defiant was a forgiving aircraft to fly; it was particularly difficult to stall, especially in stable flight, and would give the pilot plenty of warning of impending trouble. It might not have been a Spitfire, but the 'Daffy' as she was affectionately known had its own charm. At least for the pilot. The air gunner may have had other ideas. The turret was incredibly cramped, and difficult to escape from in an emergency. It was hoped there would not be too many of these. But at least it was warm. The earlier models had been somewhat draughty, but this had been easily overcome and now no special flying gear was required. The rear gunner in a Defiant did not have to deal with the icy cold and abject loneliness suffered by his counterpart in a Wellington or Lancaster, men who would return on occasion with icicles hanging from their oxygen masks where the spittle had frozen.

While Lionel practised, four other aircraft carried out operations and there was some excitement for the CO. Controlled as far as possible by Biggin Hill, he lost contact with his guide and was blown off course by severe gales. So strong were the winds that he soon found himself over Ostend, where the full might of the enemy's coastal defences opened up. Radar-controlled searchlights picked him out with apparent ease, followed by a barrage of anti-aircraft fire ('flak'). Thomas pushed the throttle fully forward and dived, escaping the searchlights' deadly beams and headed for home, seemingly none the worse for his experience.

Lionel's own chance finally arrived five nights later. He had learned of his commanding officer's adventures on the 11th. He heard also the accounts of other crews, two of whom had mixed it with German fighters in recent times, and one gunner who fancied he may have winged a Messerschmitt Bf110 that came into attack burning a white light on its wing. Another crew had escaped from two enemy fighters and was lucky to make it home without being caught. It was with this knowledge that Lionel set out with Flying Officer Eric Ferguson in the turret. They arrived at their designated forward base, Tangmere, at 16.50 hours in the company of two other crews, to refuel before being sent out on patrol, taking off again at 19.25. Their operation was carried out successfully and they landed back at Tangmere at 21.10. They returned to Heston the following afternoon at 13.45 hours.

These raw facts tell us little. We can only guess what would have been going through Lionel's mind during this, his first operation, and the nervous twenty or so minutes that he flew, with his gunner engaged in his own duties. Other pilots and aircrew on their first 'op' speak of a classic combination of fear and excitement in equal measure, not so much concern that they might be killed but rather afraid that they would let the side down. In the event, Lionel need not have worried. His sortie passed without incident, but there were those within the squadron who were not so lucky.

While Lionel was on his way to the south coast, Sergeant Frederick Hawkins, a married man from Middlesex, was flying to South Cerney in Gloucestershire. He took off in the late afternoon, but by 17.00 hours, he had still not arrived and was reported as missing. An hour later, news came through that Hawkins had crashed at Little Rissington, an airfield to the north-east. He had been attempting to land but had stalled and his aircraft plunged to the ground, killing the 26-year-old pilot instantly. It was the first death since the move to night-time Mandrel operations. That same night, Pilot Officer Bartholomew McKeon, in Defiant AA570, left Heston on time, but upon landing at Bradwell Bay on the Essex coast, the undercarriage collapsed and the aircraft was badly damaged. Fortunately neither McKeon nor his gunner, Flight Sergeant G.R. Graham, was injured.

Lionel flew two further operations in February, both from the forward air base at Coltishall and both with Sergeant R. Craig in the rear turret. It was a partnership that was to endure. The two trips proved uneventful for the new crew, but one of the other new pilots found himself in the wars. On 24 February, Sergeant Reynolds was returning to Heston and had just touched down when he was forced to swerve to avoid another aircraft on the perimeter track. The severity of the move caused the undercarriage to collapse, and the heavyweight fighter flopped on to its belly. Reynolds, who had arrived with Lionel on the same day and from the same OTU, was 'undamaged' but the same could not be said for his aircraft.

The next night proved an eventful one for the crew of Defiant AA629, with Flight Sergeant G.R. Armstrong at the controls, when they were intercepted by a night fighter and engaged in a running battle. They were some 30 miles off the Dutch coast when they spotted an aircraft beneath them at 10,000ft with a light showing. Losing the aircraft in cloud, and with ice building up on the Defiant's wings, the pilot entered a shallow dive, emerging at 6,000ft, whereupon the same or another unidentified aircraft was seen above them and to the rear, and made as if to attack. Armstrong took evasive action, turning sharply to port and then starboard, with the stalking aircraft following its every move. Sergeant Jordan, the air gunner, opened fire with two short bursts, squeezing off more than 400 rounds, and their would-be assailant broke off the engagement. Although the outcome – and indeed the identity of the other aircraft was unknown – another returning crew (Flying Officer Arthur Sinton and Flight Sergeant Leonard Johnson) told of the dropping of flares in the combat area and the Navy later reported seeing an unidentified aircraft falling into the sea.

The poor weather that had restricted the flying programme for much of February improved in March, but only slightly, allowing Lionel to fly four operations. On 1 April he lined up with the other pilots and crews for a parade to commemorate the twenty-fifth anniversary of the foundation of the RAF. The formalities were followed by another tradition – a formal luncheon served to the airmen by the officers and senior NCOs.

Tragedy hit the squadron on the night of 3 April, involving one of the more experienced crews – pilot Harry Whitmill and his air gunner Flight Sergeant Hugh 'Digsy' Moule – so called because he lived off base in 'Digs'. Having spent the morning on an air firing exercise and taking a ten-minute night-flying test in the afternoon, Harry and Digsy set off on patrol, alive to the possibility of action. They had been stooging around the night sky for more than an hour and a half when they were given a specific course to steer for home, which unbeknown to either of them would take them straight through a barrage-balloon defence. Somebody had blundered badly. Before Harry was able to realise what was wrong, there was a sickening scraping of metal upon metal as the Defiant's wing struck a steel cable. The effect was catastrophic, Harry immediately losing control of the aircraft and ordering Digsy to take to his parachute. Digsy hesitated, until Harry shouted at him to get out, at the same time insisting he would not be far behind.

Then just as suddenly as the collision had caught them unawares, the aircraft caught fire. Harry wrenched back the cockpit canopy, unbuckled his safety harness and dropped out, losing one of his flying boots in the process. Harry remembers the parachute cracking open above his head, two swings and then hitting the ground with a thud. Catching his breath, he stood up as a number of men approached, and reached into his pocket. Assuming he was searching for a cigarette, one of the men offered him a smoke, to which Harry said in true Brylcreem style: 'No thanks I'm looking for my comb!'

Harry was happy and lucky to be alive; he had baled out at around 700ft, and it was a miracle that his 'chute had time to deploy. But his good humour at his own survival was short-lived. Soon after, he learned that Digsy was dead. Although he had made it out of the aircraft in one piece – a difficult task for a Defiant gunner – he may have struck his head on the Defiant's tail, as his parachute never opened. Harry would later act as a pallbearer at his friend's funeral six days later in Bishop's Stortford, shocked and with a sense of guilt at his own survival.

The squadron's bad run of luck continued on 11 April when eight crews were detailed for operations. One of the eight was Pilot Officer Bartholomew McKeon, with Eric Ferguson – with whom Lionel had shared his first operation – in the back. They had flown Defiant AA417 up to Coltishall in the early evening and taken off again at 21.25 hours to be controlled into their patrol area. They had the misfortune, however, to be spotted by another aircraft also in their patrol area, but this time hostile.

Unteroffizier Handke, the radar operator for Unteroffizier Georg Kraft of 12/NJG1, received 'blips' on his Lichtenstein airborne radar set that suggested a heavily weaving aircraft flying off Den Helder. Handke issued a series of instructions to his pilot, closing the gap from a range of 1,800m until they were right on top of it, at which point the pilot opened fire. It took only one short burst to send the Defiant, and its crew, plunging into the sea and to their deaths. Another Defiant pilot, Flight Sergeant Robert Preston, was flying close to the scene and reported seeing an enemy fighter in the area. It is believed it was the aircraft of Unteroffizier Kraft.

April proved a busy month for Lionel and Craig, chalking up a further eight operations, four in the space of six nights. For their fourteenth operation, on the night of 24 April, their first aircraft went unserviceable (u/s) and they were obliged to take another. Despite the early hiccough, their duty was successfully carried out.

Some exciting news had reached Lionel's ears on the 23rd. The squadron had received an official signal to advise them that they would be re-equipping with a new aircraft. Their loyal if somewhat accident-prone and battle-weary Defiant IIs were to be replaced by an aircraft from the Bristol Aeroplane Company that was designed with the principal intention of being a long-range night fighter: the Bristol Type 156 Beaufighter. The 'Beau' as she was popularly known was a very different beast to the Defiant, although its performance was broadly similar. Both the Defiant II and the Beaufighter II – the aircraft they were destined to receive – took advantage of the Rolls-Royce Merlin xx, giving them a top speed comfortably in excess of 300mph. Service ceiling was also comparable, but where the Beaufighter really won was in its range and in its firepower. Whereas the Defiant had a range of around 500 miles, the Beaufighter was capable of three times that distance, making it ideal for deeper penetration raids into enemy air space. It also packed a punch, with four 20mm Hispano cannon fixed beneath the forward fuselage and – depending on the mark – a further six .303 machine guns in the wings. Lionel and the other pilots had only been trained to fly single-seat aircraft; flying an aircraft with two engines was a different prospect altogether.

News that the squadron would be receiving Beaufighter IIs was not greeted with universal enthusiasm, however. Sam Thomas, for one, had been aware of the proposed change for some weeks and had written to his superiors at Group (in a letter dated 31 March 1943) to ask them to make every effort to find Beaufighter Is or VIs in preference to the Merlin-powered IIs. He was also somewhat dubious of the plan to equip the aircraft such that they could have either Mandrel or Moonshine fitted, and that the two systems could be 'easily interchangeable'. There was talk of dividing the squadron into a 'Moonshine Flight' and a 'Mandrel Flight', and he doubted whether this would work in practice.

It would be some weeks before the new aircraft arrived, however, and in the meantime the squadron carried on with its patrols and the number of accidents continued to rise. Few were the fault of the pilots, and the accident that befell Robert Preston on the afternoon of 26 April could not be attributed to the aircraft either, but rather the weather. Returning to Heston from West Malling, Flight Sergeant Preston was taxiing the aircraft in 50mph winds when the aircraft spun around in the gales and the port oleo leg collapsed. The subsequent inquiry found that the pilot was not to blame, but the aircraft was out of action for some time.

Lionel and Craig flew an uneventful fifteenth operation on the night of 27 April, all eight aircraft detailed for operations that night touching down safely. Lionel returned to Heston the following morning. The squadron flew two more sorties in April until heavy rain prevented any further operations in strength, although a handful of aircraft operating from Tangmere managed to complete their Mandrel flight on the last night of the month and came back to base the next day.

The month of May started with the exciting arrival of a new aircraft, an Oxford II from 116 Squadron. The excitement was not so much around the aircraft itself – the Airspeed Oxford was by no means a remarkable aircraft – but rather what its appearance signified: the start of what would be a long and intensive conversion programme from one- to two-engined flying. No one was going to let Lionel (or any other pilot for that matter) loose on a Beaufighter until he had mastered something rather more benign. And with a top speed of around 200mph, the 'Ox Box' was more of a lady than the Defiant, but shared the Defiant's trait in that it would not tolerate a sloppy landing.

The first ten days of May started slowly; the 'April' showers struck with a vengeance. Conditions had improved sufficiently by the 12th to allow Lionel to fly another op with Craig from the forward base at Coltishall, followed by a further sortie three nights later, this time from Tangmere. During the latter, Harry Whitmill – now paired with a new gunner – almost came to grief on returning to Heston from a night-flying test, when the port wheel tyre burst causing the aircraft to swerve and the undercarriage to collapse. The aircraft was badly damaged but Whitmill jumped out and flew in a different aircraft to Coltishall for the night's operation, flown by pilot Sergeant Ken Slade Betts instead.

On 16 May the squadron was asked to provide a Mandrel screen for operations that night, and three machines were dispatched to Coltishall, three to West Malling, and two to Tangmere. Later that evening, however, the three machines at Coltishall and one at West Malling were stood down. The four remaining aircraft completed their operation without incident, the last one landing shortly before one in the morning. The date, though, is significant. In the late evening of 16 May, the first of nineteen specially modified, specially equipped Avro Lancasters took off from Scampton for probably the most famous bombing raid of the war – the attack on the Möhne, Eder and Sorpe Dams in Germany. It is interesting to consider to what extent, if at all, that 515 Squadron, in its own small way, contributed to the ultimate success of the raid.

An accomplished operation on the night of 19 May was followed by a most unsatisfactory affair two days later; 21 May was a poor night in more ways than one for the squadron. The three aircraft and crew sent to Coltishall, which included Lionel, were instructed not to take off, and two other aircraft suffered mechanical failures, meaning that their operations were also abandoned.

Flight Sergeant Thomas Macaulay was only thirty minutes into his flight from Tangmere when he found himself in trouble and radioed for help. It was not clear what was wrong, but it was obviously serious enough that he asked for an emergency homing. The aircraft was in some kind of distress, but whether through a fault with the engine or through enemy action was not communicated. Only a few minutes after being given the fastest route home to the closest airfield, other crews and the controller heard a 'May Day' call followed by a few sentences of confused chatter that appeared to suggest that both pilot and crew were going to abandon their aircraft. The transmissions ended after the pilot was heard to say: 'Going now. OK.'

The ground controllers assumed that both pilot and air gunner had baled out, and since subsequent attempts to contact the pilot failed, a search was immediately mounted. Boats and aircraft steered to the last known location of the Defiant, hoping to see a flare or some indication that the crew was still alive. Despite being on the scene quickly, there was no sight of either aircraft or crew, and in the darkness they were obliged to call off their search until morning.

At first light an air-sea rescue launch was dispatched, and was soon joined by five sections of two Spitfires each from 167 Squadron, all hoping to spot the tell-tale signs of debris and oil, or the yellow smudge of a life raft or Mae West bobbing in the sea. Late in the morning the launch found a flying helmet, floating forlornly in the grey swell, and when they fished it out they could read the name 'Wager' written inside. It was the name of the missing air gunner, Sergeant Geoffrey Wager. Later still they spotted part of the undercarriage and a wheel, and it was assumed that either the pilot and the air gunner had baled out too late, or for some reason they had been unable to bale out at all and had been carried to a watery grave along with their aircraft. Either way, it was a terrible way to go, and a shock for Lionel and his friends.

Two replacement crews arrived a few days later on 23 May, on the same day that Lionel and Craig were obliged to abandon a proposed operation owing to trouble with their R/T. A week later the squadron received another official signal. It was on the move.

515 Squadron in early 1943. The CO, Samuel Thomas is seated centre. Lionel is second row from the back, dead centre. Harry Whitmill is back row, second from left. Reg Dunbar is fourth from left, third row from front.

Chapter 6

A Strange Existence

Heston had been a comparatively happy home for the squadron and there were mixed feelings at having to leave. It was clear, however, that the role of the squadron was destined to change again. They had been told they would be re-equipping with long-range night fighters. An Airspeed Oxford had arrived to assist with the conversion process. Flight Lieutenant Edward Shepherd had also been seconded to the squadron, as an expert on the 'Beau'. Meantime, however, the 'day job' continued; the move was not allowed to interrupt operations any more than it had to.

Heston had been an airfield steeped in history. Officially opened in 1929 to coincide with the King's Cup Air Race, the airfield quickly became a major centre for all things flying, from private flying events and air displays, to more public demonstrations of new aircraft types. It was frequently used as the starting point for long-distance flight record attempts, notably by the Honourable Mrs Victor Bruce for her 'round the world' solo flight. Along with Croydon, it became one of the first of four airfields chosen by the British Government to serve London, and a considerable investment was made in new runways and buildings in keeping with what then constituted a 'modern' airport. It was from Heston that the British Prime Minister Neville Chamberlain flew to Munich in September 1938 and returned with his infamous scrap of paper that declared 'Peace in our time' – a peace that was to last less than twelve months.

With war came a new role for the airfield. Long before the arrival of 515 Squadron, it had initially been a base for a clandestine photographic unit and later as home to a specialist flight (1422 Flight) formed under the command of the famous pre-war flyer and test pilot, A.E. Clouston.

The Flight carried out a range of experimental trials, and it seemed somehow appropriate that 515 Squadron with its Moonshine and Mandrel equipment had shared its facilities (although this had more to do with practical issues regarding servicing and maintenance).

Hunsdon, on the Hertfordshire/Essex border, was a somewhat different proposition. Work had not begun in turning the former hunting estate into an airfield until October 1940, when the bulldozers and heavy machinery of George Wimpey & Sons moved in to start flattening the earth and constructing the runways. Responsibility for the airfield's buildings was given to a firm from Luton, but issues over the speed and quality of build led to a new contractor being appointed and delays in the project. By the time it was finally completed in March 1941, there was sufficient accommodation for more than 700 RAF and WAAF personnel, and it was a worthy satellite to the permanent field at North Weald.

Its provenance as a night-fighter base, however, was virtually without equal. Early in the war it had played host to 85 Squadron, one of the best-known exponents of night fighting, which had experimented with all manner of aircraft and equipment, including Douglas Havoc light bombers equipped with Airborne Interception (AI). It had also been home to various experiments, including the Turbinlite trials being undertaken by 530 Squadron, and that were coming to an end just at the time that 515 Squadron arrived. (Turbinlite was a searchlight carried on board an aircraft. It turned the host aircraft into an enormous flying torch that would illuminate German aircraft at night and so aid their destruction. The experiment, needless to say, was not a success.) The station was under the command of Wing Commander Hamish Kerr, AFC – a regular air force officer and previously commanding officer of 264 Squadron, the first unit to be equipped with the impressive De Havilland Mosquito.

The move to Hunsdon was completed with practised efficiency and clockwork timing. The aircraft were all flown in before midday, and the last of the squadron's ground crews and equipment in the rear party arrived late in the evening in time for the unit to be placed on operational readiness. They were indeed called for operations but subsequently stood down, although not before they had proceeded to their forward bases, Lionel among them. Lionel flew back to Hunsdon, only to fly out again in the early evening to Coltishall where his aircraft remained on the ground, the victim of the appalling weather. In the event only two out of the eight aircraft successfully completed their operations that night: four were grounded by weather; one returned early with a glycol leak; and another cut short its patrol when it lost radio contact with the controller. It was not the start they were looking for.

Weather played havoc with all operations over the next few days, the squadron only able to send up its aircraft in ones and twos. This did not prevent the squadron from taking part in a formation flying display over Haileybury as part of the school's 'Wings for Victory' parade, the boys no doubt staring up in awe as the Defiants thundered over the quad as the cadets awaited inspection from a senior visiting officer. That evening the weather improved sufficiently for Lionel to fly down to Tangmere and complete a two-hour patrol, landing in the small hours of the morning. He repeated the exercise the following evening.

When not operating, Lionel was allowed off base to drink at any one of a number of local watering holes or, when given a forty-eight-hour pass, would make his way home to north London. Longer periods of leave enabled him to catch up with friends and news from home. Tony Rosen had qualified as a wireless op/air gunner and was now at an OTU, pending a posting to a conversion unit or direct to a squadron. Leslie Israel had returned from the United States at the start of the new year and, like Lionel, was now undertaking secret work on a special squadron that he could not talk about. Peter Alexandra, John Causton, and his namesake Jack Anderson, were also all doing well, and all destined for – or already flying – heavy bombers. He doubtless reflected on those carefree days in the desert under the burning Arizona sun that must have seemed a lifetime away from the leaden skies and green fields of the Hertfordshire countryside.

Flyers lived a strange existence compared to most military men. Soldiering, it was often said, was around 90% boredom and 10% being scared out of your wits. With flying, there was constant danger: from the weather, from the enemy, and even from your own aircraft. But at the end of every flight you returned home to a pint of beer and a warm bed, and a chat in the Officers' or Sergeants' Mess about the one that got away.

Operating at night added to the levels of stress and the men coped in different ways. Harry Whitmill, for example, never flew without a lucky mascot, in his case a small white plastic elephant. His sister recalls a time when Harry was on leave and the strain was evident on his face. She remembers when he once called to say that his mascot was missing, and perhaps he had dropped it in the garden on his last leave. She did not stop looking until she had found it, and recalls his relief at her discovery.

Death was never easy to take. On bomber squadrons, whole crews would go missing in a single night; one moment they were there, the next their beds would be occupied by new faces – faces that would not be given names unless and until they had survived longer than the previous crew. In a smaller squadron, with only twenty or so pilots and air gunners, the loss of a crew was perhaps more keenly felt; more personal.

While Lionel was away, the squadron lost another crew to a tragic accident. Flight Sergeant Frederick Steel was returning to Hunsdon from Tangmere in the company of another Defiant flown by a senior officer, Flight Lieutenant A.A.S. Law who had only recently been posted to the unit having recovered from being wounded. (Law, a Canadian, had been shot down by flak while flying a Ramrod operation with Hurricane-equipped 32 Squadron. By all accounts he had been lucky to make it home alive.) The two aircraft became separated in fog and pressed on independently for home. Law arrived safely, but Steel soon became overdue. News subsequently reached the squadron that an aircraft had crashed into hills near Beachy Head, and both pilot and gunner – Pilot Officer Albert Gray, DFM – had been killed. Gray had only recently been commissioned, having survived a near-fatal crash two years earlier as a wireless op/air gunner with 83 Squadron. Indeed, until his death he had lived a charmed life: he had been awarded his DFM for a tour of thirty-two operations in 1941; he had also flown in the first two of Bomber Command's 1,000-bomber raids while 'resting' at an OTU prior to joining the Defiant Flight. It was experience they could ill afford to lose.

Another significant incident during this period was the arrival on 11 June of the first of the Rolls-Royce-powered Beaufighter Is, and the pilots were keen to get to grips with their new charge. For the time being, however, they were obliged to stick to their current duties and aircraft, and technical troubles continued to frustrate the squadron's operational efficiency. The very next day, as if to drive the message home, of the three Defiants dispatched to Coltishall, one suffered a collapsed undercarriage, one had to return with engine trouble, and the third failed to take off owing to a high radiator temperature. New aircraft could not come soon enough, and over the next few days two variants of another twin-engined aircraft – a Bristol Blenheim – arrived to swell the ranks of training aircraft and accelerate the conversion process.

Lionel and Craig returned to operations on the night of 17 June, the start of a busy few days for the crew that saw them complete five operations in a little over a week. On the night of 25 June, Lionel was at the end of a long operation where he had been airborne for more than two hours when he lost contact with his controller. He was not unduly concerned; it was perfectly possible to navigate his way home without assistance, and in the event he was helped by friendly searchlights which 'homed' his aircraft to Bradwell Bay and safety. It was with some relief that he climbed out of the cockpit after more than two and a half hours in the sky – his longest sortie to date.

That night, contact was also lost with another aircraft flying from Coltishall, Defiant AA572. Unfortunately, the aircraft disappeared at about the same time and in the same location that 500 or so heavy bombers were on their way to attack Gelsenkirchen, a popular 'oil' target in Germany, and so no plot for the machine could be seen on the Operations Room table. It had, in effect, vanished in the confusion of a main force raid. By early the next morning it was clear that some harm had come to the aircraft and its crew – Flying Officer Arthur Sinton and Pilot Officer Leonard Johnson. As soon as the aircraft was known to be overdue, a search was instigated by the air-sea rescue but no trace of the Defiant, its pilot or the air gunner was found. It was a sad demise of two very experienced men. (The aircraft was probably shot down by Oberleutnant Heinz-Martin Hadeball (12/NJG4), who claimed to have intercepted and shot down a 'Hurricane' over the North Sea off Westkapelle. The body of P/O Johnson washed ashore near IJmuiden.)

The squadron had little time to consider its loss. While Johnson's body was later recovered and interred in a cemetery in Amsterdam on 17 July, there was no such Christian burial for Arthur Sinton. He had no mortal remains to honour, and his name was added to the thousands of airmen who have no known grave, and whose memories are perpetuated at the Runnymede Memorial.

July started much as June had ended, with questionable weather and further frustrations with unserviceable machines and equipment. Lionel fell foul of two different aircraft both experiencing trouble with their R/T sets, such that by the time he finally arrived at Tangmere, he was too late to take part in any operations.

Better luck followed; Lionel and Craig completed two trips on 6 July and 7 July but ran into further difficulties on the night of 8 July. They had flown down to West Malling and sent off on patrol at 23.20 hours. Twenty-five minutes later, however, they were obliged to return when the pitot head – the essential piece of equipment that determined the aircraft's air speed – snapped off. Without an accurate idea of speed, a pilot could easily stall the aircraft and crash, especially in bad weather conditions that involved fog or heavy cloud where a pilot could quickly become disorientated, even to the point of not knowing whether his aircraft was the right way up. Several pilots had flown into the ground, convinced that they were climbing when they were in fact in a dive, and with no ASI (air speed indicator) the risk was just too great. Lionel returned to West Malling and landed, one of five squadron aircraft obliged to abandon their duties thanks to the weather or mechanical failure. Lionel's aircraft remained at West Malling until it was repaired.

By now, Lionel and Craig were two of the most experienced members of the squadron, having chalked up more than twenty operations – some fifty hours of dangerous and exhausting combat flying. The RAF oper-ated a system of 'tours', rotating aircrew so they did not become burned out, understanding that a weary pilot was at greater risk than one who was refreshed after a six-month rest from operations. A tour was not an exact science and changed over the course of the war. It also varied depending on the command. A tour in Bomber Command, for example, comprised thirty operations, after which aircrew were rested – usually at an OTU – and then required to return for a second tour of twenty ops, after which they could not be called back for a third. A tour in Fighter Command was not based on operations, but rather on the amount of combat hours flown – typically 200 hours for day fighters and 100 hours for night fighters. Coastal Command crews in their long-range flying boats flew a tour comprising 800 hours.

The system was intended to reflect the risk, maintain operational efficiency, and foster higher morale. Aircrew had to believe that they could and would survive if the odds were on their side. Interestingly, the percentage odds of coming through a first tour of operations in Bomber Command (at the end of 1942) was almost directly comparable to the odds of surviving a tour in Fighter Command (44% versus 43%). Night fighters were considered more risky (crews had a 39% chance of survival) and crews in long-range fighters had the best chance of making it through in one piece (c. 60%).

Lionel and Craig were an accomplished and effective crew who had, in effect, grown up, and the squadron had matured with them. The number of crews now steadily began to increase, and the shape and make-up of the squadron started to change. Squadron Leader Sam Thomas, DFC, AFC, a stalwart servant of the squadron, and its commanding officer from the outset when the squadron had simply been a Flight, was posted back to Heston in the short term, to continue experimental flying. He had been a popular commanding officer – an easy-going man who was not too much of a disciplinarian and preferred to command authority by leading from the front. It had earned him the respect of his men but now it was time to hand over the reins. The 'establishment' of the squadron had officially been transformed, and the CO position elevated to that of a wing commander, a rank above squadron leader. And now the squadron comprised two full Flights – 'A' and 'B'. A new man arrived to take over, Wing Commander James Inkster.

Inkster, from Birkenhead, had apparently been reading medicine at Oxford before the war. He had rejoined the RAF at the beginning of 1939, having originally been appointed to a commission in 1934 before being placed on the Reserve. He was a regular officer with regular views.

The difficulties with the Defiant's undercarriage continued to plague the pilots of 515, and Harry Whitmill in particular. On his transit to Coltishall for operations on the night of 13 July he found that one wheel could not be lowered and he returned to Hunsdon to await further instructions. He flew over the airfield several times to allow the squadron engineer officer to assess the problem and give him the best advice. The EO recommended that Whitmill retract the undercarriage and crash-land. Happily, on his last pass, Harry was able to get both wheels down and locked and landed without further incident. He was too late, however, to take part in that night's operations.

An unusual incident occurred on 17 July. Lionel was operating that night and returned to Tangmere after two hours of stooging up and down the enemy coast without provoking an adverse response. He reported no sign of enemy activity on his return. But the enemy was certainly out there, and accounted for another of the squadron's more seasoned crews. Flying Officer George Walters took off from Tangmere five minutes after Lionel, and set off over the English Channel to take up his station. Walters, an Australian, was not flying with his regular air gunner as he had a cold, and so had taken Warrant Officer George Neil in his place. Both pilot and replacement gunner failed to return.

Unusually, however, their demise had been witnessed not only by their vanquisher but also by other, less-hostile aircrew flying that night. Flying Officer Cyril Bennett was in a Mosquito XII of 256 Squadron on a defensive patrol out of Ford, an RAF base on the south coast. He had already been bloodied in combat, destroying a German Dornier 217 only a few weeks earlier. Now he was on the hunt for further prey, and spotted what he thought was a friendly aircraft going down in flames about 10 miles ahead of him. He raced to the scene, alert to the danger, spotted a radial-engined Focke-Wulf 190 close by and engaged. It was one of Germany's best fighters and in the hands of a skilful opponent could prove deadly, but this one was no match for our night eagle. With a single burst he shot the fighter down and returned with grim satisfaction to base. It was assumed that his victim was in turn the victor over Defiant AA651, the mount of Walters and Neil.

At dawn the following morning, a search was instigated by the air-sea rescue, joined by Lionel and Craig. Lionel took off at 06.00 hours and searched the area where the Defiant was reported to have ditched but saw nothing. It was unusual to find a downed aircraft and crew in the sea, even when the location had been accurately fixed. With his fuel gauge falling, Lionel was obliged to call off the search and returned to Hunsdon with a heavy heart and nothing but two and a half hours of flying time to record in his logbook.

If the dangers of Mandrel operations were not already apparent to the crews of 515 Squadron, the events of the next twenty-four hours showed just how dangerous their secret world was becoming. While the new wingco flew over to Tangmere to learn more about the loss of his men, eight Defiants were being readied for operations that evening. The usual fifteen-minute night-flying tests were undertaken before the eight crews set off for their forward bases: two to Tangmere, three to West Malling and the balance to Coltishall.

It is unclear whether Lionel was flying that night (the Form 540 that details flight operations is mysteriously incomplete), but if he was not, then he had chosen a fortunate night to sit one out. The first crew to encounter trouble was flying Defiant AA381. The pilot, Sergeant Hubert Louden, and his air gunner Sergeant Tingle were about an hour into their flight and were patrolling a little way off the Dutch coast. All was well until the pilot suddenly saw what he quickly identified as a Focke-Wulf at a height of around 6,000ft and 500ft distant. At that range, and with a closing speed of 600mph, it was obvious that the fighter would be on them in a trice, and Louden kicked at the rudder bars and moved the stick in his hands to take violent avoiding action and make his Defiant a difficult target at which to aim. The Fw190, which had caused panic in the ranks of the RAF fighter squadrons when it first appeared in August 1941, screamed over the top of Louden's Defiant, missing his rotor blades, it seemed by only inches, before banking to port. Tingle had no time to fire off his guns and when the aircraft was next in sight, it was heading towards the safety of cloud and the Dutch coast. The crew resumed their patrol, none the worse for their encounter.

Ten minutes later, Pilot Officer David Foster was similarly a little over an hour into his patrol when he spotted something light brightening the night sky above him, flying east. It was an unidentified aircraft burning its navigation lights, a practice often favoured by German night fighters but which could easily be a German bomber returning from a night raid on England or even a British bomber with an absent-minded crew on its way to attack Germany. Either way it passed without incident, though later in the flight Foster reported that an airfield, possibly Flushing, was illuminated no fewer than six times, long enough, probably, to allow an enemy aircraft either to land or take off. Foster might have wished at that moment that he was not at the controls of a Defiant, but rather a Beaufighter or one of the newer De Havilland Mosquitoes that were now wreaking havoc across Holland and northern France.

The closest shave of the night, however, went to the crew of Defiant AA375 from West Malling. Pilot Flight Lieutenant F.J. McGarry and air gunner Flying Officer Simmonds, a senior-ranking crew, were coming towards the end of their operation when the gunner spotted an unidentified single-engined aircraft only 500ft away at a height of around 4,000ft. Taking no chances, the pilot immediately threw his aircraft into a steep turn to port and watched to see what happened next. The unknown aircraft followed him in the turn, at which point the gunner opened up, firing a short burst from all four of his Browning .303 machine guns, the distinctive smell of cordite from the spent cartridges filling his turret and his nostrils. The air gunner kept his eye glued to the aircraft, which he was sure by now was hostile, and watched it turn away to port and make for what little cloud cover was available. Despite excellent visibility, both pilot and air gunner soon lost visual contact with the fighter and it did not return.

All of the squadron's aircraft returned home safely next morning.

After the excitement of its penultimate operation, the final operation for July passed as something of an anticlimax, especially as it was the very last operation that the squadron would fly for some time. Bad weather prevented them from getting airborne and then a direct order was received from Fighter Command to cease all operations forthwith. The reason for the order was not given, which caused some excitement in the NCOs' Mess that evening, as the pilots and air gunners considered their destiny over a tankard or two of beer. The wing commander returned from a brief spell of leave to try and ascertain more, but seemingly without any luck. Meantime, Lionel and his squadron pals waited, spending what little breaks in the weather there were to practise formation flying and increase their hours of twin-engined dual control on the aircraft available. A lucky few had already progressed to the Beaufighter and were full of praise for the new machine.

A clue to the intense nature of their flying and the strain it placed on the men's bodies and minds is given in a simple entry in the squadron Operations Record Book (ORB) for 1 August. Flight Sergeant Craig, Lionel's faithful and long-standing air gunner, was sent away – not on leave or to another unit, but rather to Dutton Homestall Rest Centre, a country house on the outskirts of Ashurst Wood in Sussex. Dutton Homestall had been used by the RAF since the beginning of the war as a rest home for exhausted aircrew, as well as a recovery centre for those 'guinea pigs' that had been badly burned and patched up by the pioneer plastic surgeon, Archie McIndoe. Craig was not the first, and he would not be the last, to take advantage of its peaceful surroundings, to recoup and remuster his strength for the battles ahead.

By 8 August, news had got round that the night-flying sorties were now over, and that 515 Squadron would be resuming daylight operational work at some time in the future. Moonshine was back on the agenda. For the time being, however, the unit was declared non-operational. Lionel had survived his first tour. Official confirmation followed the week after when the wing commander, along with his engineering officer and special signals officer, attended a conference at the headquarters of 11 Group and learned their fate. What it all meant in practice was still unclear, but the conversion to 'Beaus' suggested long-range fighter work, and new pilots were posted in to swell the ranks and assume leadership roles, among them Squadron Leader Joseph Cooper as a flight commander.

Promotions also followed within the squadron. Lionel was appointed a flight sergeant, and earned a modest increase in pay accordingly. More importantly, he was able to put up a 'crown' above his sergeant's chevrons. Craig, already a flight sergeant, was promoted to warrant officer, the highest rank available to a non-commissioned officer but one that entitled him to be called 'Mr Craig' – an affectation that doubtless caused considerable amusement to his pilot.

Sam Thomas was also recognised with further command, this time of 3 Squadron flying Hawker Typhoons, a sturdy fighter with proven ground-attack capabilities that would later prove instrumental in harrying the German Army across the fields of Normandy.

The squadron was yet to rid itself of its Defiants and reliability was still a major headache. The manufacturers, Boulton & Paul, offered to assist, and following a visit to their factory in Wolverhampton, the squadron received the assurances they needed that expert help was on hand if required.

The vacant flight commander's post was filled on 6 September with the arrival of Squadron Leader John Shaw, who was posted in from 62 OTU, a unit that trained radar operators for the night-fighter force. Indeed, the next few weeks were filled with training that combined both day- and night-fighting skills, from Airborne Interception (AI) tests to air-to-air combat training, punctuated by air-to-ground and air-to-sea firing drills. As well as live ammunition, they also fought mock duels using cine (camera) guns to record who had shot down whom. The films were played back to the crews after the event, and were often subjected to ribald commentary.

September morphed into October and then into November with more of the same. Lionel grew accustomed to the routine. Low flying became the order of the day, the crews skimming over the Hertfordshire countryside and at the allocated ranges as low as they dared, a portent of what was to follow. They also practised flying with one engine; two engines left more margin for error but were not immune from danger. Knowing how to fly and indeed land on one engine could ultimately save a pilot's life, and the life of his observer. Lionel would learn this lesson perhaps sooner than he imagined.

There were other duties to perform. The recently promoted Flight Sergeant Anderson took off in Defiant AA418 in the evening of 21 October to stooge around for an hour or more while friendly searchlights endeavoured to find him in the dark. Such 'co-operation' flights, as they were known, were incredibly tedious for the pilot, but essential training for the hard-working searchlight crews. Lionel had a new gunner in the back, Flight Sergeant Rowe.

Still the precise role for the squadron had not been determined, or if it had, then it had certainly not been communicated to the crews, who were somewhat in limbo. In early November, the machine guns in the turrets of the Defiants were all harmonised at 400yd (effectively this meant that the .303 rounds from each gun would converge on an area 400yd distant, concentrating the rounds in the hope of inflicting maximum damage). The work was undertaken in readiness for day operational work. The wing commander was forever backwards and forwards to 11 Group HQ with his engineer officer and signal officer in tow, and new aircraft (Beaufighters) began to arrive in quantity – five in the space of two days – along with new crews from recently established Tactical Exercise Units (TEUs).

As well as instruction in the air there was also instruction on the ground, especially during spells of bad weather, of which there were plenty. Few pilots ever thought they would die, and if they were shot down many assumed they would evade capture by outsmarting the wicked Hun. It was known that some pilots even went prepared, not just with the escape kits that were standard issue but escape equipment of their own making. At the start of the war, after the German occupation of northern Europe, airmen had little chance of evading capture before being picked up by German forces. But as the war progressed, and the Resistance movement became more organised, a few men did get home and the numbers increased. Dedicated evasion lines, separate from the Resistance, were established to help shot-down RAF (and later USAF) aircrew, passing men down the line from safe house to safe house until they could be escorted over the border into neutral Spain.

The pilots and crew of 515 Squadron were briefed on escape and evasion and given clear instruction on what to do if brought down over enemy territory. They were to avoid the temptation for human contact unless and until they were sure that the contact was friendly, and even then they were to be cautious. They were to hole up during the day and only travel at night, and avoid busy roads, rail junctions and bridges as far as possible. The advice was given to them by an evader with first-hand knowledge of what it was like to be shot down and on the run, and they listened intently to his experiences.

After weeks of comparative inactivity and uncertainty, events now began to unfold quite quickly. Towards the end of November the squadron received a most distinguished visitor, an air commodore by the name of Addison and from a group that no one had heard of. It wasn't surprising. The group had only been in existence for a handful of days and its role was still top secret.

Air Commodore 'Eddie' Addison had served in the Royal Flying Corps in the First World War as a mechanic, and was commissioned into the newly formed RAF in 1918. After the war he had gone up to Cambridge to study natural sciences, and although he returned to Service life in 1921, he continued to study, his appetite for learning being one of his many remarkable qualities. He became somewhat of a specialist in electronics. A professional airman, he had first come to a modest degree of prominence for his involvement in the Battle of the Beams in command of 80 Wing. The Germans had been experimenting with radio guidance to steer their bombers on to the target, and Addison and his teams had done everything in their power to stop them, with some notable success.

Now he had been given command of 100 Group with a mission to harness the various disparate airborne and ground-operated radar units, homing and jamming equipment and radio countermeasure (RCM) technologies then being deployed in the secret war against the Germans, and bring them together into one, unified command structure. The group would also have a wider role in 'bomber support' – controlling various squadrons of deep-penetration Mosquitoes to seek out and destroy enemy night fighters and their airfields ahead of the bomber 'stream'.

It was perhaps more with this latter role in mind that the air commodore met with the 515 Squadron CO, and the pair were joined by Addison's deputy, Wing Commander Roderick 'Rory' Chisholm. Chisholm already held the DFC for shooting down seven German aircraft at night, and was one of the first and the very best night fighters that the RAF had produced. His weapon of choice in those early days had been the Beaufighter and there was little or nothing he did not know about the aircraft or how to get the best out of it. He had been 'rested' as commander of an experimental night interception unit and his experience was much sought after by the powers that be.

Yet another different make of aircraft arrived on 29 November, a Bristol Beaufort – an aircraft more familiar as a torpedo bomber. It came with its own pilot from RAF Honiley, Flight Lieutenant E.M. Ramsey, to assist with dual instruction. The Beaufort had derived from the Blenheim and shared several similarities, but was much heavier (it was designed to carry a crew of four) and therefore slower.

Lionel was among the first to give it a try, having first read through the essential Pilot's Notes and talked through the controls and the aircraft's handling characteristics with his instructor. After flying single-engined aircraft for so long, to Lionel the cockpit seemed so much busier and the aircraft much more complicated to fly. It was an interesting choice for a learner pilot, given that contemporaries described the Bristol creation as being difficult to fly and prone to mechanical failure. Happily, Lionel's first taste of dual instruction in the Beaufort passed off without incident, and a few days later he was given fifty minutes of ground instruction on the Beaufighter, courtesy of the wing commander himself. Although it is not recorded, Lionel flew solo soon after, and built up his flying hours as time and the weather allowed.

He knew now that the squadron was embarking on a new episode in its life, an exciting one in which it would earn much praise, but also one fraught with dangers. For Lionel, these dangers would ultimately take his life.

Lionel's burial stone with the Star of David prominent. The inscription reads: 'Mourned by his beloved parents and his brother Gerald. We will remember him.'

Chapter 7

Intruders

A secret cypher was received by the squadron administrative office on 7 December from the recently re-formed HQ Air Defence Great Britain (ADGB – a name to which the former Fighter Command had reverted), instructing the squadron to move. But this was not just a relocation to a new station within the group, or even within the command. The squadron was being transferred from 11 Group to 100 (Special Duties) Group, part of a whole new unit: Bomber Command.

In view of the imminent move, the first of the Defiants was finally struck off charge. The squadron no longer had need of their services, and the faithful old warhorses were at last being retired, if only temporarily. No doubt they would re-emerge as target tugs or instructional aircraft. Three were dispatched to Reid & Sigrist, an instrument manufacturer in Desford that also served as a maintenance unit (MU); sixteen were sent to 10 MU and six to 1692 Flight.

With the aircraft gone the men busied themselves in the now well-rehearsed packing of their equipment, stores and personal kit to take with them to Little Snoring, a quaintly named RAF station in Norfolk that had only recently opened as a satellite to Foulsham. A movement control officer arrived and provided detailed arrangements regarding freight and rail accommodation for the journey. An advance party left by rail on the morning of 13 December and arrived that afternoon. The main party followed two days later, courtesy of a special train laid on for the event. Lionel and the rest of the pilots flew in the same day, and by the 16th the squadron was settling in.

Christmas came and went, with the customary dinner served to the men by the officers, and in the evening all ranks attended a special concert given by a local repertory company from Norwich. On the last day of the year, Flight Lieutenant Ramsey returned to 63 OTU, his work in teaching Lionel and others to fly twin-engined aircraft duly completed.

The New Year dawned, a year of hope and expectation that the war might soon be over. Although the Second Front had not yet opened, the Germans were already fighting a battle they could not win. The Soviets were advancing in the east through the Ukraine and had liberated Kiev; British and American forces were approaching the Gustav Line in Italy; and the *Scharnhorst*, one of the ships that Lionel had teased his father about in his letters, had finally been caught and sunk off the North Cape.

More new equipment was being assessed by the wing commander, including Serrate, a new and innovative radar detection and homing device that could latch on to the equipment used by German night fighters and find them in the dark. Its only shortcoming was that it could not detect the range of the aircraft it had found, but that could be overcome by combining Serrate with the latest mark of AI, and showing the contact information on the same display tube. It would be a potent weapon in the operations that were to come.

Lionel flew a number of local practice flights during the day, but had the frustration of seeing the various night-flying programmes cancelled because of poor weather and fog in particular. The weather was especially bad on the morning of 21 January and no flying was carried out. By the afternoon, however, the conditions had sufficiently improved to allow a truncated programme to be completed by three pilots of 'A' Flight (under Squadron Leader John Shaw) while Lionel (part of 'B' Flight under the command now of Squadron Leader R.G. Taylor) waited his turn for some night-flying practice.

There was nothing in his pre-flight checks that indicated a problem. The ground crew cleared for him to taxi, and Lionel released the brake catch on the aileron control hand wheel and the aircraft started to roll. Taxiing to the main runway, he reapplied the brakes and waited patiently for the green signal from the Aldis lamp in the control caravan. When good to go, he checked the throttle controls and dials, released the brakes, straightened the tail wheel and eased the throttles forward to allow the aircraft to build up speed. Lifting the tail wheel by applying forward pressure on the control stick he waited until the aircraft had sufficient speed before pulling back on the control column to lift the main wheels clear of the deck.

Waiting a few moments until at a safe height and clear of any potential obstacles, Lionel raised the undercarriage and flaps and again watched the dials as the Beaufighter climbed at a constant speed of around 150 knots. The most critical part of any flight is the take-off and landing, and just at the moment that Lionel was beginning to settle in to his flight the starboard engine cut out. Now he was in real danger. Until that moment he had never really stared death in the face, but this time he was on his own. The advantage of having two engines was that you could still fly with one, and they had practised for this very eventuality. But even with training Lionel still lacked experience, and the aircraft and its flying characteristics were still unfamiliar to him.

Lionel ran through the emergency routine, balancing the aircraft as best he could against the now dead weight of his useless engine. The controls felt heavy in his hands as he fought to maintain level flight. Pilots were always told never to turn back to the field with a dead engine straight after take-off. The aircraft would stall and fall out of the sky. Lionel heeded this advice and only turned once he was certain he had sufficient air speed and control to conduct the manoeuvre safely.

He called the control tower over the R/T to report his condition, and was given immediate clearance to land. Conducting a complete circuit of the airfield he turned to start his final approach, continuing to fight the controls but aware that he needed to get both his wheels and his flaps down if he was to make a safe landing. He selected the undercarriage lever and also notched down 15 degrees of flap, but both too early and with insufficient speed. Unable to maintain height, and with the nose at an alarming angle, the aircraft flopped on to the ground with a spine-shattering thud and a scraping of metal. The Beaufighter skidded on its belly, a few vital yards short of the runway, only just reaching the perimeter track where it came to a sudden and dramatic stop.

For a moment there was a stillness and quiet in the cockpit. Then realisation of the danger dawned. Lionel was dazed and bruised from the straps biting into his shoulders, but otherwise unscathed. He fumbled hurriedly for the red lever to his right and pulled it, thus jettisoning a part of the canopy window, and bundled himself out just in the nick of time. As he scrambled to his feet to run, there was a whoosh of air and rush of heat as the aircraft burst into flames. Moments later the fire tenders and the 'meat wagon' (ie an ambulance) arrived to take the hapless pilot for a check over in the sick bay. Remarkably, Lionel appeared none the worse for his experience, but possibly wiser. He would remember next time – if there were to be a next time – not to be too eager with his wheels and flaps.

Taylor, Lionel's flight commander, was with the squadron only briefly before being posted. A few days after that, on 26 January, there was an even more significant move: the appointment of a new CO.

Inkster had performed his job well, overseeing the squadron during a difficult time in its transformation. But with its role now more clearly defined, a new type of commanding officer was required, one with direct experience of intruder-style operations. His name was Wing Commander Frederick Lambert.

Fred Lambert was a Canadian who went by the imaginative nickname of 'Cordite'. Remarkably he had originally been in the Naval Reserve and travelled to the UK to attain an apprenticeship in the Merchant Marine, but somehow had been tempted away by the lure and excitement of flying. He joined the RAF in 1936 and began operating on the North-West Frontier, being mentioned in a dispatch for his work in taming the rebels at Waziristan before the outbreak of the Second World War. He remained in India for some time, flying Blenheims and Lysanders (a high-wing single-engined monoplane) with 20 Squadron before moving to command 110 Squadron with Vengeance dive-bombers. He returned to the UK in March 1943, and after further conversion and operational training arrived at 141 Squadron as a flight commander. He had modest success with 141, claiming a Bf110 as damaged while flying a Mosquito II in December, before receiving notice that he was to take over at 515 Squadron.

Lambert continued where Inkster left off, with more flying training to bring the crews up to scratch and integrate new personnel into the squadron. For a few days the two wing commanders worked together to ensure a smooth transition of responsibilities and power.

Although the new airfield sounded a little sleepy, there was perhaps rather too much excitement for one or two of the crews to cope with in their first few weeks of occupation.

Flight Sergeant Louden, for example, was stooging along quite happily one morning in an Airspeed Oxford on an instrument flying test to Hunsdon when he caught a glimpse of what he took to be a fire in his peripheral vision. Turning his head to the left he had the somewhat unnerving sight of a small tongue of flame licking itself around the port mainplane. Keeping calm, but obviously in a state of anxiety, Louden coaxed the aircraft home and landed without further incident, without the fire spreading to any dangerous degree. The fire tenders were immediately on hand to extinguish the flames as the Oxford rolled to a halt, and all was well. The cause of the fire was not obvious; it was decided to leave it to the Air Investigation Branch to worry about.

Three days later, on the first day of February, Wing Commander Inkster and Flight Lieutenant Law were on air-sea rescue duties (100 Group had laid down that two Beaufighters were on constant standby for ASR) when Law's aircraft developed engine trouble. Although it continued running for a brief period it finally petered out when only 15 miles from the Dutch coast. Law had a rather hairy journey home across the Channel and, as Lionel had discovered to his cost, was unable to maintain height and crash-landed at Orfordness. Neither pilot nor navigator was injured.

The AOC 100 Group stepped in midway through the month to rule that the Merlin-powered Beaufighter IIs that were still in the squadron's employ were no longer to be used for practice cross-country exercises at night, and found two Mk VI Beaufighters from 1692 Flight to fit the bill. A Mk I was also flown in the next day.

A decision had been made, however, that the squadron was not to be equipped with the Beaufighter for much longer. Intruder squadrons were all being 'standardised' on to the De Havilland Mosquito, and so arrangements were made for 141 Squadron and 169 Squadron each to 'lend' 515 Squadron one of their Mosquito Mk IIs to assist with training. It was yet another exciting development for Lionel and his friends, and they could not wait to get to grips with an aircraft of which they had heard so much about but had as yet to fly. The Mk II was a pure fighter version with a top speed of more than 360mph and a range of more than 780 miles.

She could fly faster, further and higher than anything Lionel had ever flown so far, and he was keen to make a start.

Training intensified throughout February, as the weather allowed, with a further Mosquito being flown in from West Raynham to accelerate the programme. Addison was clearly in a rush to get another intruder squadron into the war to support the bomber effort. He ordered that four Mk IIs were to remain on the squadron pending the delivery of the variant that the unit would ultimately fly in combat, the fighter-bomber (FB) Mk VI.

At the end of February, Lionel said goodbye to a good many of the squadron stalwarts who had given such sterling service but whose job was now done. Nearly all of the air gunners were posted out, many to 192 Squadron to provide further bomber support in larger aircraft carrying radio countermeasure (RCM) equipment. Others were sent to be rested at OTUs all across the country, including Warrant Officer Craig, dispatched to 12 OTU, a bomber operational training unit at Chipping Warden. Most of the pilots stayed, their numbers bolstered by a dozen or so new faces, all to be joined by a group of more than thirty navigators. Among the new pilots were several with previous operational experience, the most notable among them being Squadron Leader Robert Moore, DFC. Moore had completed a tour with 11 Squadron and won his DFC for a daring attack on shipping on Beirut Harbour in the summer of 1941, by which time he had already completed thirty-five operations. An expert exponent of two-engined aircraft, Moore was appointed to command 'B' Flight, and therefore effectively became Lionel's new 'boss'.

A new month arrived and the training schedule showed no sign of relenting. David Foster, who had survived a close shave with a German fighter off the Dutch coast the previous summer, found himself in trouble again, partly of his own making. While coming in to land after a thirty-minute night-flying exercise he made a normal approach and touch down but then attempted to use his port rudder to correct a swing to starboard and found that the rudder was stuck. The aircraft skidded sideways off the runway and the port wheel was torn away. This placed more strain on the undercarriage, which finally gave in to the inevitable and collapsed, damaging the port engine cowling and wing tip. Miraculously, Foster lived to fight another day and survived the wrath of his commanding officer, who had made it clear that anyone who pranged one of his kites would be immediately posted. An investigation into the incident found that the rudder had become stuck after the collapsible ladder, used when pilots were landing away from home, had come loose from its mounting. 'Cordite' let Foster off with a warning and ruled that ladders were no longer to be taken on board aircraft unless completely necessary, and the war continued. (Tragically, David Kay Foster was to be killed in action on 28 May 1944.)

Lionel knew that operations could not be far away now, and his hopes were accelerated when the CO and his navigator were seconded to 605 Squadron at Bradwell Bay to gain first-hand information and experience on the sort of work they would be carrying out. It could not have been a more perfect debut for Lambert, or indeed the squadron. On their very first operation, on patrol to an airfield to the east of Paris, they spotted what they believed to be a Heinkel 177 (a large, long-range German heavy bomber) and promptly shot it down. The aircraft was hit with a short burst and seen to strike the ground. Although there was no fire or explosion, the aircraft was claimed as destroyed and a triumphant wing commander returned to base, fully satisfied with his night's work. It was precisely the sort of start the squadron had been waiting for.

The Mosquito Mk VI aircraft began arriving throughout March, coming in twos and threes from various groups, maintenance units and even straight from the manufacturers in Hatfield, until it had reached its agreed complement of sixteen plus two in reserve. Meanwhile, the practice flying in the remaining Mk IIs continued, as did the incidents and accidents that plagued any wartime squadron. Flight Lieutenant Stanley Hoskin was the latest to hit trouble, when his Mosquito's port undercarriage collapsed on landing for no apparent reason, causing the aircraft to loop on to the grass. Luckily he was unhurt. The Mosquito, it seemed, shared some of its idiosyncrasies with the Defiant when it come to staying on its feet.

Squadron Leader Moore, the 'B' Flight commander, was the next to follow his skipper to 605 Squadron but did not share the same luck, having to abort his practice mission with a faulty compass. They had more fortune the next day, although they returned with little to report from their travels across northern France. The 'A' Flight commander, and CO while Lambert was on leave, also joined 605 Squadron for the day but similarly arrived back empty handed.

April arrived predictably wet. Lionel had only three weeks to live.

The trend towards sending pilots and navigators to 605 Squadron on attachment for so-called 'freshman' sorties continued and Lionel, despite his experience, had to wait patiently for his turn. Meanwhile, those who had already been 'blooded' in combat were ready to undertake the squadron's first official sorties from Little Snoring. These started on 7 April with a flight of four aircraft, led by Lambert, and comprised his two flight commanders and another flying officer by the name of 'Eric' L'Aime who had only recently arrived on the squadron. Lambert's winning start could not be repeated, and all four Mosquitoes returned with little to show for their endeavours.

The dangers of flying at night were plenty. Judging one's height at low level was especially difficult. Pilots and navigators worked as a team, the navigator keeping a close eye on the altimeter and calling out the height as they descended. Both would also keep a keen look out for enemy aircraft, flak positions, and any other dangers that might be lurking in the dark. Sometimes that meant their own aircraft, as one of the squadron pilots found to his horror on the night of 9 April. Flight Sergeant Angus Stein was flying at 500ft when he spotted what he took to be a four-engined Lancaster only 300ft above him. What a Lancaster was doing at such a height is difficult to say, since it put them in danger of light flak. Perhaps it had been hit; maybe the pilot had consciously brought his aircraft so low to avoid fighter attack. Whatever the reason, it was not alone. Only moments later, another four-engined 'heavy', this time a Handley Page Halifax, was also passed at 800ft, no doubt giving both crews the fright of their lives. The young Scotsman returned without further incident, chastened somewhat by his experience.

That same night the squadron suffered its first casualties of the year, and indeed since it began its new sphere of operations. Sadly, one of their most experienced pilots was killed – Harry Whitmill. The squadron had actually been released that morning until 12.00 hours on account of 'the continual night work for the past week' (according to the ORB), and to give the ground crews a rest. Seven aircraft were detailed for operations that evening, and in the late afternoon Harry took one of the Mosquitoes on a night-flying test. Shortly before midnight, Harry and his 21-year-old navigator, Flying Officer David Biggs, left Little Snoring with a brief to patrol the area of Paris/Lille and hunt out enemy fighters. No one knows what happened, beyond that their aircraft failed to return. Both men were originally buried near to where their plane fell, between Coulommiers and Solers, and later reinterred in the cemetery at Villeneuve St Georges. It was unfortunately not the only casualties they would sustain that month.

On the night of 26/27 April, the squadron operated at near maximum capacity, putting no fewer than thirteen aircraft and crews into the air. The C-in-C Bomber Command had ordered a major raid on Essen involving almost 500 aircraft. The nightly strength of the RAF heavy bomber force at this stage of the war comprised more than twice that number, and 'Butch' Harris also called for two smaller attacks on Schweinfurt and Villeneuve St Georges.

The most senior pilot flying in 515 Squadron was the wing commander whose aircraft was armed with fragmentation and incendiary bombs as well as cannon and machine guns. The intention was to cause maximum damage to aircraft, buildings and men on the ground, to confound and destroy. Lambert took pleasure in depositing his ordnance on the airfield at Quakenbrück, home to various day- and night-fighter establishments as well as a major aircraft repair and overhaul facility. He then headed for home.

Warrant Officer Thomas Ecclestone, a veteran Defiant pilot, had an even better night. Detailed to patrol St Trond, one of the most famous of German night-fighter bases (home at one time to Heinz Wolfgang Schnaufer, Germany's leading night-fighter ace, nicknamed 'the Night Ghost of St Trond'), he arrived to find the airfield in darkness with not a light showing, so decided to move on. He made for Le Culot in Belgium where he struck gold. He could see quite clearly ahead of him an enemy aircraft coming in to land. Sliding in behind it, unseen, he opened fire at a comparative long range of 800yd, closing with a three-second burst at 300yd and seeing his cannon and machine-gun rounds strike home, dancing on the aircraft's fuselage and wings. Then it burst into flames.

With the lights on the airfield now extinguished, and the only illumination coming from the downed aircraft, Ecclestone slipped away in to the night and made for the coast via Brussels/Evere. Here he was in luck again, for he immediately spotted an enemy aircraft with its identification lights showing, and again swung into attack. On this occasion he timed it such that the aircraft had just touched down and was rolling along the runway, blissfully unaware of the imminent danger behind. Ecclestone opened fire at 500yd and the reaction was immediate, a mass of flames breaking out from the doomed aircraft. Then all hell let loose with the searchlights and flak probing the sky, desperate to avenge their dead colleagues. Ecclestone made for home. Two confirmed kills in a single night was enough for any man.

Meanwhile, another of the squadron's new arrivals was having the time of his life. Squadron Leader Harold Martin, DSO, DFC, had caused quite a stir when he arrived on the station. Not for his blond hair, moustache, or Australian drawl. Not even for his chest full of medals, including the sought-after 'double' of the Distinguished Service Order and Distinguished Flying Cross. Everybody knew 'Micky' Martin, for his face and name had been plastered all over the national press twelve months earlier as one of the Dambusters, the men of 617 Squadron who had destroyed the dams in Germany and won everlasting fame, respect and immortality. But Martin was mortal, and he yearned for operations. Now he found himself in control of one of the most potent weapons the RAF had in its armoury, and doing what he loved best: flying as low as he dared and causing mayhem.

Martin had been given Venlo on the Dutch/German border as his target, and arrived a little more than an hour after take-off to begin his patrol, keeping his eyes peeled for a slight movement in the night that might betray an enemy aircraft. With not much happening at Venlo he pushed on to Wesel and Bonninghardt where he dropped a few bombs on the funnel lights for want of something better to do. He proceeded to hunt around, finding little of interest before returning to Venlo to discover the runway lights had been switched on. Spotting an aircraft that had just landed, he swooped in with cannons blazing, closing from 600 to 300yd, damaging the fighter that he identified as a twin-engined Junkers 88. He saw more aircraft in the circuit but was not able to press home his advantage and so moved on again, this time to the airfield at Gilze-Rijen where he followed another aircraft in to land and dispatched it with a two-second burst that prompted a flash and a red glow. He headed for home, his work complete.

Lionel was also flying that night, in the company of Sergeant Anthony Sims, a young navigator who had only been with the squadron for a little over two weeks. He had only recently completed his training at 22 OTU at RAF Wellesbourne. The pair had taken their turn at 605 Squadron in the company of two other crews a few days earlier, and now were on operations for real. They too had been ordered to patrol Venlo, and to see what transpired. Shortly before one o'clock in the morning the pair clambered through the bottom hatch of their aircraft, Mosquito NS895, and settled themselves in for their pre-flight checks. The cockpit was cramped, which was both a hindrance and an advantage: a hindrance for it left little room to manoeuvre, especially for the navigator; an advantage, because the proximity of the pilot and navigator allowed for better communication.

Switching on the ignition and pressing both the starter and the booster coil buttons while the ground crews worked the priming pump, the engines readily burst into life with a reassuring growl. Lionel checked the temperatures and the pressures, and that the various hydraulic-driven surfaces were performing satisfactorily. Taxiing around the perimeter track while testing the brakes, Lionel and Anthony ran through the checklist for take-off: trimming tabs; propeller; fuel; flaps. With the brakes released, and the engines roaring, Lionel kept the Mosquito straight on the runway, countering the tendency for a slight swing to port by opening the port throttle slightly ahead. Raising the tail wheel by a light forward pressure on the control column, the Mosquito effortlessly climbed into the air, Lionel selecting the undercarriage 'up' and checking for two green lights. At an indicated air speed (IAS) of 148 knots, the aircraft began to climb into the dark, and the airmen settled in to their routine, with a long night ahead.

The Mosquito had sufficient fuel for more than four hours' flying, although various factors could both extend or diminish their reserves. At 05.35 hours Micky Martin came in to land, the last of the crews to return and a full thirty minutes after the Mosquito of Flight Sergeant

Terrence Groves and his navigator had landed after a fruitless search for enemy aircraft. (He would have more luck on future sorties, and indeed go on to win the DFC as a pilot officer.) As the minutes became hours, Lionel's aircraft was listed as overdue. Phone calls were made to see if his plane had landed away. It was a frequent occurrence when a returning aircraft was low on fuel, or perhaps battle damaged. Crews were questioned by the intelligence officer but had seen nothing. Lionel was missing.

In the ORB the simple words were typed by the adjutant: 'This aircraft being detailed to patrol Venlo aerodrome took off from Little Snoring at 00.55 hours and has since become overdue and is reported missing. Nothing was heard from this aircraft after take off.'

The squadron's practised administration then swung into action. A telegram was dictated and sent to Lionel's parents. They all followed a similar script: 'We regret to inform you that your son, Flight Sergeant Lionel David Anderson 1388016 is missing as a result of air operations on 27th April stop. Any further information will be immediately communicated to you stop. Pending receipt of written confirmation from the air ministry, no information should be given to the press. OC 515 Squadron.' The same telegram, with the appropriate name change, would be sent to Sergeant Sims's parents.

The next day a letter followed, written – or at least signed – by Lambert's hand. It spoke of Lionel's loss as though it were a personal affront: 'I held your son in the highest esteem, more especially as I have heard of the sterling work he has performed since he joined the squadron. He was popular with his comrades.'

Later, much later, details would emerge of what happened to the crew of Mosquito NS895, which had come down near Deelen, a few kilometres to the north of Arnhem. Both men had been killed. Perhaps they had found nothing at Venlo, and decided to look elsewhere. Deelen was a well-used and well-defended Luftwaffe air base and a legitimate target. Whether Lionel was shot down by flak, or whether he misjudged his height in the darkness may never be known, but the outcome was the same nonetheless.

The squadron received a signal the following morning from the AOC, 100 Group: 'My congratulations on an excellent night's work. Now that you are well bloodied may you have good hunting and plenty more to come.' Sadly for Lionel his life was fully spent.

Gerry Anderson (left) with the older brother he idolised.

Chapter 8

The Thunder Birds Legacy

The mortal remains of Lionel are buried at the Arnhem (Moscowa) General Cemetery on a hill to the north of the town on the Apeldoornseweg. Perhaps appropriately it adjoins the Jewish cemetery. He is one of thirty-three Servicemen buried in the peaceful grounds.

News of his death was quick to make the pages of the *Willesden Chronicle* but it was not, in fact, until March the following year that Lionel, who was originally reported 'missing', was finally presumed killed – almost twelve months after he had been shot down. The wait had been interminable for Joe and Debbie, and so too for his little brother Gerald. While an airman was still only 'missing' there was always the hope that he might yet turn up alive, perhaps having been hidden by the Resistance or somehow on the run and unable to make contact. 'Presumed killed' had more finality. Doubtless the advancing Allied troops had overrun his original place of burial, and had notified the relevant authorities.

Lionel had loved flying, a fact made clear in his letters and the subsequent reminiscences of his brother who distinctly recalls the day when Lionel flew low over his house in a Mosquito, to thrill his younger sibling with the roar of the Merlin engines. It left quite a lasting impression.

As an airman, Lionel was no doubt disappointed to have come through more than a year of training only to find himself flying the outdated, outgunned warhorse that was the Defiant. But the aircraft served him and the squadron well, and their work was invaluable. Of course, it did not have the same glamour as flying a Spitfire or Typhoon, and neither did it seem to attract the same awards, but its contribution to the air war should not be underestimated. In a lengthy report dated June 1943, while the future of 515 Squadron was being decided, there is an interesting passage that states that there was 'real evidence' to show that both ground-based and Defiant-based Mandrel had a tangible impact on reducing Bomber Command's losses. The minute also went on to detail recordings from the local resistance fighters that showed that ground Mandrel, *but more especially Defiant Mandrel* (author's italics), was 'a considerable nuisance to coastal Freya stations'.

It is difficult to look at Bomber Command's losses for the period and draw any definitive conclusions. Like for like comparisons are virtually impossible because the numbers of sorties undertaken rose dramatically in that time. Between January and July 1943, the period in which airborne Mandrel was being deployed, RAF Bomber Command dispatched 35,447 aircraft on night-time operations and lost 1,298 bombers to fighters, flak or causes unknown. Between January and July the year previously, Bomber Command sent out 20,771 aircraft and lost 766.

The figures do not perhaps tell us much; the actual loss ratios are virtually identical, but they do demonstrate a dramatic increase in Bomber Command operations during that time. Perhaps the fact that the percentage loss did not rise, despite the increased sophistication of the German defences and the increased experience of the German night fighters, hints at the impact that Mandrel and 515 Squadron may have had at keeping the losses in check. Doubtless Lionel's view, and the view of the squadron at that time, was that if they helped save a dozen or so crews, then their efforts would have been worthwhile – and there is every suggestion that they did.

So how dangerous was it to fly in a given patrol area, at the dead of night, in an accident-prone and often unreliable aircraft, knowing that at any moment you could be stalked, detected, and shot down by a German night fighter with only your wits, your flying skills and your four Browning machine guns for protection?

We can only guess how Lionel felt, but someone who knows, and someone who was there can help us better understand. Reg Dunbar was an NCO air gunner with 515 Squadron, who flew both Moonshine and Mandrel operations. Reg arrived on the squadron with plenty of experience already under his belt, having miraculously survived two tours as a rear gunner – some fifty ops – at a time when many didn't make it through their first half-dozen. He and the other air gunners were sent initially to Drem in Scotland, to train. They were also dispatched to Malvern in Worcester, to be instructed by the scientists of the TRE on the 'special' equipment that was to be installed in their aircraft.

Reg remembers: 'For our daylight operations (Moonshine) we would fly in formation at about 12,000ft with our Spitfire escort at 15,000ft. When we were near the coast, we would switch on the transmitter so that the Germans saw us, allowing the RAF or USAF bombers to take off on the "real" raid. As soon as we knew the Germans were in the air, the pilot would turn the aircraft around, put the nose down and return to base at sea level.' At night, he explains, the dangers were greater still: 'It was a very edgy business. In the morning we would fly to our forward base to refuel. Then we would take off individually and make for one of ten or so specific positions off the enemy coast. When we reached our patrol area, we would switch on the equipment to jam the German radar, just at the time that the Main Force of bombers went out or was due back.'

While Mandrel was switched on, communication with their controller was lost: 'There was a danger of interference, but the danger to us was that our controller could not warn us if there were enemy aircraft in the area. We were on our own. It was not unusual to get back and find one of our number was missing.'

'We had a dual role as gunner and equipment operator,' Reg continues, 'and there was not a great deal of room in a turret, especially when, like me, you are six feet one! When it was time to operate the jammer, I would have to drop the bench-like seat that we sat on and squeeze down inside the aircraft fuselage to switch the equipment on. While all this was going on, remember, we were effectively totally defenceless. I was not at my guns, and no one could warn us if there were any enemy fighters about.'

The air gunners were not only absent from their turrets to flick a switch. Their role was to find the relevant Freya frequency, and ensure the needle on the 'dial' was constantly in place, to make certain a continuous 'jam' was maintained. 'This meant being absent from our guns for 20 and sometimes 30 minutes while we were on station, meaning that at any moment we could be "jumped" by an enemy fighter, with no means of fighting back.' Reg believes that the majority of the losses to enemy fighters occurred while the air gunner was busily engaged with the

Mandrel equipment. Certainly those who were shot down appeared to have been taken by surprise.

In addition to the German fighters, Reg had other close shaves. Searchlights, he says, were always 'hairy', but the Defiant's reliability also gave cause for concern: 'I was once flying with an Australian – George Walters – who was not a very experienced pilot and half way across the channel his voice came on the intercom to say we had a glycol leak. That meant that soon the engine would begin to overheat and ultimately it would stop. He asked me what I thought we should do? There is no point being brave when you have an engine overheating so I simply told him to turn back. ... On another occasion I was due to fly with George again but had a heavy cold and was grounded. He took a different gunner with him, George Neil, and the pair of them failed to return.'

Reg, who is ninety-three at the time of writing and retired as a wing commander, comes from a generation who continually understate their achievements and the full extent of the dangers they faced. He flew with no fewer than twenty-three different pilots during his tour with 515 Squadron – a risk in itself – including a very brief night-flying test with Lionel in October, after the squadron had been stood down from operations. Reg seldom flew with the same pilot for more than a handful of trips because of the casualty rate. George Walters, Arthur Sinton and Thomas Macaulay were just three who were in the driving seat while Reg sat in the back with his guns and his box of tricks, and all three were killed in action while flying with different crew.

For Reg to describe Mandrel operations as 'edgy' in the context of all of his previous operational experience gives the reader some idea of just how perilous they must have been. It also gives further insight into the dangers that Lionel faced, albeit that he was fortunate to have had the same gunner for almost all of his operations, which undoubtedly contributed to his survival.

The role of 515 Squadron has never been fully documented, and there is a tendency in previously published material to confuse Moonshine and Mandrel, even though both performed very different tasks and presented contrasting risks. More has been written about the task of intruding, but detailing its hazards seems somehow superfluous given that Lionel appears to have been shot down on his first ever. If ever proof were required of its dangers, then surely Lionel's death tells us all we need to know. (According to Martin Middlebrook, author of *The Bomber Command War Diaries*, by the end of the war, 515 had flown some 248 operations for and in support of Bomber Command, comprising 1,366 individual Mosquito sorties. It lost 21 aircraft (1.5%) but on the plus side accounted for 11 German aircraft destroyed in the air, 18 on the ground, and 5 more damaged on the ground. Perhaps most significant of all, it suffered the most losses and highest percentage loss of all 100 Group Mosquito squadrons.)

So what of Gerry Anderson, and the legacy that Lionel's death left behind? Some excellent biographies of Gerry have already been written but certain facets of his life are worth highlighting. Gerry followed his brother into the RAF, albeit long after the war was over, and as part of his obligatory National Service. He had by then already abandoned any hopes of becoming an architect in favour of working in films, and when interviewed by the RAF education officer was sent to the Radio School at Cranwell from whence he was posted to RAF Manston in Kent. Two incidents had a profound impact on the young man. One involved a tragic accident during a flying display to commemorate the Battle of Britain when a Mosquito crashed out of control into a group of spectators, killing twenty. Not long after, while Gerry was working in the control tower, he heard a message that an aircraft was coming in to land with a damaged undercarriage. After a tense approach, relayed with an equally dramatic commentary, the pilot managed to bring the aircraft down in one piece. Both incidents can be linked directly to Gerry's first ever *Thunderbirds* story, 'Trapped in the Sky'.

But the RAF influence generally, and Lionel's legacy specifically, goes back further and deeper than a simple storyline. Gerry was devastated by his brother's death. His mother, Debbie, was heartbroken too. Indeed, it is said that she never recovered from the tragedy of losing her eldest and most beloved son. It is even suggested that in her grief she once cruelly remarked to her youngest boy that it should have been him who had died, and not Lionel, and that Gerry would never be able to match the achievements of his elder brother. The story has passed down the ages and in all likelihood is true. People say cruel things when overcome with the pain of losing someone so dearly loved, and the words would have had a profound effect on a young teenage boy who was also grieving for the brother he worshipped. It is thought that Gerry's uneasy relationship with his mother is the reason that few, if any, strong 'mother' figures appeared in any of his puppet works. The Tracy family, for example, features a father – Jeff – and his sons Scott, Virgil, Alan, Gordon and John, but no mother. A similar comparison may be seen in *Joe 90*, with the close bond between father and son, and not a mother in sight.

Perhaps the first influences, however, can be seen in Gerry's initial foray into the genre with which he became synonymous: *Supercar*. *Supercar* pre-dates *Thunderbirds* and featured a vertical take-off and landing craft piloted by the dashingly heroic Mike Mercury. In the programme's first ever episode, the Supercar crew save the passengers of a downed private plane, and among those rescued are young Jimmy Gibson, his older brother Bill, and his pet monkey Mitch. The pair are invited to stay with Mike and the Supercar inventors at their secret hideaway in Nevada.

It has been suggested that Mike Mercury is a character inspired by Lionel Anderson: the heroic pilot, battling against the odds. Mike sees Jimmy as a younger version of himself, and like Mike, Jimmy loves aircraft and building model planes. Bill Gibson, meanwhile, is Jimmy's older brother who is always absent, and always leading an exciting life, joining the air force and even NASA. The mix of characters, personalities, life experiences and relationships are all closely interrelated. Mike as the daredevil test pilot might easily be Lionel, but so too Bill Gibson, the older brother, somehow just out of reach and leading an exciting life, just as Lionel did in Arizona. Jimmy, meanwhile, was one of many orphans that Gerry would feature in his stories and that might easily reflect on his own life, dispatched as an evacuee early in the war and living – in part at least – a miserable early childhood. He was the complete opposite of his brother: introverted; quiet; shy. In the background; not one for the limelight.

Mike Mercury and Scott Tracy, the equally heroic pilot of Thunderbird One, are two peas from the same pod. Whereas it would go too far to link Scott Tracy directly to Lionel, the inferences and references are there once again. Gerry was never a pilot, and never a hero, but he always cast his lead characters in that mould, whether riding a Supercar, flying a Thunderbird, or diving a submarine in the case of *Stingray*.

Stephen La Riviere, an acknowledged expert and author of *Filmed in Supermarionation – a History of the Future* had the good fortune to interview Gerry on a number of occasions, and said that Gerry never once formally acknowledged that *Thunderbirds* or indeed any of his puppet series' characters were influenced by Lionel. Subconsciously, however, the influences are there. Gerry was always in wonder and awe of aircraft – caught up in a fantasy world perpetuated by his brother's tales of derring-do in the air, and apparent in his early letters home. This doubtless manifested itself in the outstanding creativity that Gerry demonstrated in vehicle design for his leading 'men'. A more subtle reference may be seen in Tracy Island. Debbie Anderson always kept an enormous portrait of Lionel on the wall – a portrait that became a focal point for all who visited. Might that, subconsciously, have been the reason for the five portraits of the Tracy boys that adorned the walls of Tracy Island?

There has been some discussion over the years as regards how *Thunderbirds*, Gerry's most famous creation, came to get its name. Most have suggested that Gerry was prompted by Lionel's references to Thunderbird Field in his letters. It is indeed true that Southwest Airways intended to call the third of their airfields 'Thunderbird Field III' but they never did. More importantly, Lionel never mentions Thunderbird Field in any of his letters home, although he does talk at length about the propaganda film in which he took part, and which dominated their lives for the few weeks of filming. The logical conclusion is that Gerry simply 'mis-remembered' in good faith, and as such the story soon became established as fact. Stephen La Riviere again cites several examples where Gerry's memory played tricks on him, and history has been effectively rewritten as a result.

Lionel's life in the shadow of Hollywood, socialising and even dancing with some of the greatest names in cinema at that time and being shown around the famous film sets must have been bewitching to his younger sibling. The glamour contrasted dismally against the depressingly grey life of war-torn London and is difficult – seventy-five years on – to imagine. But it undoubtedly left its mark on an impressionable young Gerry, and again must have contributed to the path he was eventually to take into film.

Gerry, it was said, would never match his brother's achievements; they would never be sufficient to fill the frame in which his brother's portrait once hung. Lionel was the all-action hero; the pilot, popular with his friends, good with the girls. Gerry spent his entire life trying to be as good as his brother, to live up to him, and yet, ironically, it is Gerry who is known the world over and Lionel who is recalled simply as a footnote in his younger brother's history.

Both, however, deserve to be remembered. Both should now never be forgotten.

Dramatis Personae

Peter Alexandra

George Peter Alexandra, always called 'Peter', was born in Newcastle on 24 March 1922, the son of Arthur and Helen Alexandra from Tickhill in Yorkshire. His parents must have travelled for he was educated at Slough Grammar School, and after graduating from university he moved to Billingham to work as a research chemist with ICI. While at ICI he enlisted in the RAF and found himself on his way to train at Mesa as part of Course 7. Returning to the UK he joined Bomber Command, and by January 1945 was a flight lieutenant with 170 Squadron operating from Hemswell. He completed half a dozen operations with the squadron before his aircraft was shot down on a raid to the synthetic oil installation at Bottrop on 3 February, and all of the crew were killed. They are buried at the Reichswald War Cemetery on the Dutch border.

John Thomas 'Jack' Anderson

Commissioned upon gaining his wings, Jack was shot down and killed on 20 October 1943 as a flight lieutenant. He was the pilot of a Lancaster II of 115 Squadron, detailed for operations to Leipzig. His aircraft failed to return. He was later shown to be the victim of a German night fighter flown by Leutnant Paul Fehre. It was the German pilot's second victory.

Bob Barter

Graduating as a sergeant pilot, Robert Barter was later commissioned. He was promoted war substantive flight lieutenant in August 1944, after which no further service details have been traced.

Geoff Bullen

On successfully graduating from Course 7, Geoff Bullen was one of the few to be commissioned (Pilot Officer 127906). He became an instructor, and did not return to the UK until later in the war. In May 1944, he was attached to 1665 Heavy Conversion Unit (HCU) at RAF Tilstock. He flew Short Stirlings, and on the night of 5/6 June was one of the pilots responsible for towing Horsa gliders packed with British paratroopers for the attack on the bridge over the River Orne, a raid made famous in the classic war film, *The Longest Day*. He towed more gliders into Arnhem in September, as well as taking part in a number of resupply drops to the beleaguered Red Devils. With 570 and 196 Squadrons he flew numerous operations in support of the Special Operations Executive (SOE) in Holland, Denmark and Norway. After the war he continued to fly and became a gliding instructor. He died at the age of ninety-one in April 2014.

John Causton

John Causton was born in Greenwich in London on 13 August 1923 and volunteered for service in the RAF at the first opportunity. He was one of the youngest to be trained in Mesa, and was still only a teenager when he was awarded his wings, a few days shy of his nineteenth birthday. He was commissioned on 7 August 1942, shortly before embarking on his journey home. John joined Bomber Command, flying with 102 Squadron, and in December 1943 was awarded the Distinguished Flying Cross, the citation running as follows: 'On every occasion, Flight Lieutenant Causton has pressed home his attacks with vigour and determination. His objectives have included such heavily defended targets as Berlin, Hamburg and Essen. In August 1943, while over Berlin, the port outer engine of his aircraft failed but by his skillful [sic] airmanship, he flew back to base and landed safely with only three engines functioning. This officer has the complete confidence of his crew and has proved to be an outstanding captain.' John Causton survived the war, and in 1965 was awarded the OBE, having attained the rank of wing commander. He retired in 1966 and died on 10 May 1986.

Leslie Israel

By some bizarre twist of fate, Leslie Israel was killed while operating on the night of 18 November, 1943 the same night that Tony Rosen was killed, but with a different squadron and in a different role. Leslie, from Cricklewood, had completed his flying training at Falcon Field, where he had been introduced to Lionel. Returning to the UK at the end of 1942 he was commissioned – a result, no doubt, of having attended public school at Haberdashers. Pilot Officer Israel was posted to 192 Squadron, a Special Duties squadron, its aircraft carrying early electronic countermeasures to mislead the German defences. The role was not dissimilar – again coincidentally – to that played by 101 Squadron. Leslie's aircraft, a Halifax V, took off from Feltwell at 17.45 only to be recalled less than an hour later. At 20.20 his aircraft was seen to crash 2 miles from base, but within the confines of the aerodrome. Leslie was killed along with three others. Five were injured, of whom three were to die of their injuries. Leslie's body was returned to his home town; he was buried at Willesden Jewish Cemetery.

Anthony Rosen

'Tony' Rosen was born in June 1922 and lived in Willesden Green, being educated first at Dudden Hill School and afterwards at Willesden County School. His mother left soon after the end of his schooling to live in Bournemouth. Volunteering for aircrew in August 1941, Tony qualified as a wireless operator/air gunner and was promoted to sergeant. In the summer of 1943 he joined 101 Squadron, a Special Duties squadron flying Lancasters from Ludford Magna. They carried an eighth, German-speaking crew member to operate an airborne radio jamming device known as Airborne Cigar. On the night of 18 November that year, and flying his seventh operation, his aircraft – piloted by Pilot Officer Charles McManus – was shot down on a raid to Berlin. Tony and all of the crew were killed.

Operational Record of Lionel Anderson

1943

February

16.2.43	1st op	Night operational flight from Tangmere (in AA405) with Flying Officer Eric Ferguson in the turret. Duty carried out (DCO).
18.2.43	2nd op	Night operational flight from Coltishall (in AA583) with Sergeant R. Craig in the turret. DCO.
26.2.43	3rd op	Night operational flight from Coltishall (in AA549) with Eric Ferguson. DCO.

March

3.3.43	4th op	Night operational flight from Coltishall (in AA549) with Flight Sergeant Craig. DCO.
10.3.43	5th op	Night operational flight from Coltishall (in AA435) with Flight Sergeant Craig. DCO.
13.3.43	6th op	Night operational flight from Coltishall (in AA549) with Flight Sergeant Craig. DCO.
27.3.43	7th op	Night operational flight from West Malling (in AA438) with Flight Sergeant Craig. DCO.

April

9.4.43   8th op   Night operational flight from Tangmere (in
                          AA549) with Flight Sergeant Craig. DCO.

10.4.43   9th op   Night operational flight from Tangmere (in
                          AA579) with Flight Sergeant Craig. DCO.

14.4.43   10th op   Night operational flight from Coltishall (in
                          AA572) with Flight Sergeant Craig. DCO.

16.4.43   11th op   Night operational flight from Tangmere (in
                          AA651) with Flight Sergeant Craig. DCO.

17.4.43   12th op   Night operational flight from West Malling (in
                          AA653) with Flight Sergeant Craig. DCO.

19.4.43   13th op   Night operational flight from Tangmere (in
                          AA651) with Flight Sergeant Craig. DCO.

24.4.43   14th op   Night operational flight from Coltishall (in
                          AA414) with Flight Sergeant Craig – first air
                          craft went u/s and crew transferred to different
                          aircraft – AA414. DCO.

27.4.43   15th op   Night operational flight from West Malling (in
                          AA651) with Flight Sergeant Craig. DCO.

May

12.5.43   16th op   Night operational flight from Coltishall (in
                          AA655) with Flight Sergeant Craig. DCO.

15.5.43   17th op   Night operational flight from Tangmere (in
                          AA548) with Flight Sergeant Craig. DCO.

19.5.43   18th op   Night operational flight from West Malling (in
                          AA383) with Flight Sergeant Craig.

21.5.43	–	Operation briefed but scrubbed.
23.5.43	–	Operation abandoned after twenty minutes due to R/T trouble. Duty not carried out (DNCO).
27.5.43	19th op	Night operational flight from West Malling (in AA651) with Flight Sergeant Craig. DCO.
28.5.43	20th op	Night operational flight from Coltishall (in AA655) with Flight Sergeant Craig. DCO.

June

5.6.43	21st op	Night operational flight from Tangmere (in AA655) with Flight Sergeant Craig. DCO.
6.6.43	22nd op	Night operational flight from Tangmere (in AA572) with Flight Sergeant Craig. DCO.
17.6.43	23rd op	Night operational flight from Coltishall (in AA572) with Flight Sergeant Craig. DCO.
19.6.43	24th op	Night operational flight from Tangmere (in AA572) with Flight Sergeant Craig. DCO.
21.6.43	25th op	Night operational flight from Tangmere (in AA572) with Flight Sergeant Craig. DCO.
24.6.43	26th op	Night operational flight from Tangmere (in AA572) with Flight Sergeant Craig. DCO.
25.6.43	27th op	Night operational flight from Coltishall (in AA655) with Flight Sergeant Craig. Owing to R/T trouble they lost contact with the controller and were homed by searchlights to Bradwell Bay. DCO.

July

6.7.43	28th op	Night operational flight from Tangmere (in AA655) with Flight Sergeant Craig. DCO.
7.7.43	29th op	Night operational flight from Tangmere (in AA571) with Flight Sergeant Craig. DCO.
8.7.43	–	Took off from West Malling but had to return when pitot head (which gives indicated air speed) snapped off. DNCO.
12.7.43	30th op	Night operational flight from Coltishall (in AA655) with Flight Sergeant Craig. DCO.
15.7.43	31st op	Night operational flight from Tangmere (in AA655) with Flight Sergeant Craig. DCO.
17.7.43	32nd op	Night operational flight from Tangmere (in AA436) with Flight Sergeant Craig. DCO.
		End of first tour.

1944

26/27.4.44	33rd op	Detailed to patrol Venlo aerodrome. Failed to return.

Author's note: Information is taken from the 515 Squadron ORB. It is assumed that the operation of 25 June 1943 was completed. A further 'freshman' operation is indicated in early April 1944 on attachment to 605 Squadron, but no details are recorded in the 515 or 605 Squadron ORBs.

Course 7

The following information is adapted from the summary provided by the RAF in Arizona Falcon Field, with additional research. It does not include the names of civilian trainees. Of the fifty RAF pupils on the course (including Alfred Palmer who was transferred to Course 8), exactly half were killed in action or while in the Service. The most distinguished alumni were John Causton (Wing Commander John Causton, OBE, DFC) and Flight Lieutenant Frederick Wright, DFC, AFC, although at least another five other airmen went on to win the DFC or the NCO equivalent (and rarer) DFM.

George Peter Alexandra	Killed in action with 170 Squadron, 3.2.45.
John 'Jack' Anderson	Killed in action with 115 Squadron, 20.10.43.
Lionel David Anderson	Killed in action with 515 Squadron, 27.4.44.
Norman Ballamy	Killed in action with 44 Squadron, 14.6.43.
Bob Barter	Graduated as sergeant pilot. Later commissioned.

Douglas Baxter	Nicknamed 'Tex', was shot down while flying with 155 Squadron against the Japanese but was rescued; posted to 60 Squadron (P-47 Thunderbolts); survived war. Posted to 72 Squadron (Vampires).
Geoffrey Bullen	Commissioned. Survived war.
John Causton	Distinguished bomber pilot with 102 Squadron. DFC and later OBE. Promoted to wing commander. Survived the war.
Allan Cox	Killed in service on 31.7.44 while still only twenty-two.
Leon Cramer	Commissioned pilot officer. Flew Typhoons with 56 Squadron in 1943/44.
Albert Crawford	Killed in action with 50 Squadron, 15.6.43.
H.F. Crossman	No service details traced.
A. Duckworth	Sergeant pilot. No further service details traced.
James Fraser Petheridge	Killed in action with 198 Squadron, 20.6.44.
Charles Gentry	Killed in action with 155 Squadron, 5.11.44.
Frank Glew	Killed in a flying accident, 1.4.42.
W. Gray	Graduated as sergeant pilot. Later commissioned.
Maurice Harrison	Killed in action with 614 Squadron, 6.7.44.

George Honey	Graduated as sergeant pilot. Later commissioned. Tour with 102 Squadron and then posted to 35 Squadron Pathfinder Force (PFF). Awarded the DFC.
Alastair Hope Robertson	Killed in action with 578 Squadron, 21.7.44.
John Jones	Killed in action with 108 Squadron, 8.3.44.
John Knight	Killed, 28.11.43.
Brian Laing	Killed in action with 61 Squadron, 3.8.43.
Aubrey Lens	Remustered as an air bomber. Killed in action with 75 Squadron, 24.8.43.
George Lovell	Killed in action with 78 Squadron, 24.3.44.
Charles Lyon	Killed in action on third operation with 635 Squadron PFF, 31.3.44.
Frederick Matthews	Remustered. Was still serving in 1967.
G. McGhie	Remustered.
Frederick Metcalfe	Killed in action with 619 Squadron, 31.8.43. Awarded the DFM.
John Mills	Graduated as sergeant pilot.
A.R. Mitchell	Graduated as sergeant pilot.
Jack S. Mitchell	Graduated as sergeant pilot. Later commissioned.

Hew Morrison	Killed in service at 85 OTU 27.7.44 in a collision with another aircraft. He had more than 640 flying hours to his name.
Alfred Palmer	Qualified with Course 8 and killed in action with 549 Squadron, 8.11.44.
Dennis Parker	Commissioned. Promoted to flight lieutenant.
Hamish Pattullo	Commissioned. Promoted to flight lieutenant.
Dudley Rolph	Remustered. Joined 'Y' Service.
Nicolai Schwartz	Killed in action with 29 Squadron, 17.12.44.
James Steele	Killed in service with 76 Squadron, 3.11.43.
Derek Taylor	Commissioned.
Malcolm Teasdale	Killed in service, 31.12.42.
Ron Thackray	Operations with 10 Squadron and 50 Squadron. Awarded the DFM with the former as a flight sergeant, as 'an outstanding captain whose efforts have been worthy of high praise'. Later commissioned.
Michael Thompson	Killed in action with 88 Squadron, 29.7.43.
Kenneth Tinsley	Awarded the DFM as a pilot with 150 Squadron.
Norman Veale	Killed in service with 239 Squadron, 3.8.43.
R.E. Watts	Graduated as sergeant pilot.

R.G. Watts   Remustered.

Richard Wilder   Graduated as sergeant pilot. Later
                          commissioned and awarded the DFC, serving
                          with 101 (Special Duties) Squadron.

H.B. Wren   Remustered.

Frederick Wright   Graduated as sergeant pilot. Later
                          commissioned and awarded the DFC while
                          serving with 12 Squadron (1943) and the AFC
                          in the New Year's Honours of 1946 for his
                          work at the Bomber Command Instructors'
                          School at Finningley.

Other noteworthy contemporaries during Lionel's time at Mesa
include Edward Hicks, one of only a handful of pilots to be awarded
the Conspicuous Gallantry Medal (CGM). Hicks, who qualified from
Course 4, flew operations with 466 Squadron and was recognised for
bringing his seriously damaged aircraft home after an attack on
Stuttgart. Three other members of his crew were also decorated.
He was later commissioned, and awarded a DFC. Eric Searle, another
Course 4 alumnus, was awarded a DFC as a Spitfire reconnaissance
pilot. One of his more remarkable trips was an operation from
Murmansk in Russia to photograph the German battleship *Tirpitz*
('The Beast'), hiding in the Alten fjord in Norway.

Course 6 included Richard Cleaver, a pilot who went on to fly
glider-towing aircraft, for which he was awarded the Distinguished
Service Order. He added a DFC while flying operations for the Special
Operations Executive (SOE) and made a successful 'home run' after
being shot down in 1944. The same course also featured Neill Cox,
a Beaufighter pilot who was awarded two DFCs for operations in the
Mediterranean, and after the war famously took off in a Spitfire with
a WAAF flight mechanic still perched on the aircraft's tail! Among
those to attain more senior rank was Peter Gilpin, who retired as
Group Captain Peter Gilpin, CBE, DFC.

RAF Flying School in Arizona Desert

News – Talk given by Donald Boyd
Sunday 26 April 1942 at 6pm
Home Service
BBC broadcast

In Arizona, the desert seems endless. It's broken only by eruptions of jagged rock mountains, and it's easy to understand how it came to be compared with the sea, for the mountains rise out of the waste like distant islands. The desert's mostly bare earth and stones, with tall cactus and short cactus; cottonwood trees which have foliage like grey smoke, and little puffs of grey scrub. When I was there a month ago or so, there were some flowers too, the colour of yellow charlock, with heads like dog-daisies.

But wherever the desert's irrigated, then it produces in abundance – oranges, grape-fruit, lemons, dates, cotton of course, lettuce, cantaloupe melons and apricots.

We were driving through some orange groves, full of fruit, in some of this irrigated land, when we came to a British flying school which does its work in the desert, in full view of these jagged mountains. A few miles away, there's one mountain of red rock; rock built up in slanting fiery terraces. It stands by itself on the edge of the plain, a very commanding sight; and behind it there's a distant succession of mountains, powdered with snow at the time; and on the right, there's the immense rock mass called Superstition Mountain. Its northern face ends not with a precipice, but with a reverse slope many hundreds of feet high. And below that drop there's a series of rock pinnacles. And even from 15 and 16 miles away, you can see the great vertical crevices in the body of the mountain; and the crags of its torn silhouette. And over the marvellous landscape, there's the brilliant hot sun, and sometimes, as we saw, an endless procession of cumulus clouds drifts slowly to the south. It's not much like England.

The first man we met when we came to this school was an RAF cadet who came from Blackpool. He'd only been there three days, but already he'd settled himself in; and it was he who knew the names of the mountains, and pointed out the apricot blossoms in the orchards; and he seemed to find himself quite at home.

The cadets come from all parts of the British Isles to take their elementary courses from American civilian instructors working under RAF officers. They train on biplanes during the elementary course, and then on Vultee and Harvard aircraft during their advanced training. There's all the equipment here necessary for ground training and training in the air; and the cadets' day is split up between the classroom and the air, and at the end of the course, there's an examination and the cadets are rated accordingly.

I asked one of the officers how they enjoy themselves here, so far from home. Very much, he said, once the letters from home begin to arrive. The cadets spend their free time on the airport, sunbathing or playing tennis or association football, badminton and archery – but unfortunately they haven't anybody up to Scorton Arrow standards to teach them the use of the bow, just at present. And soon they hope to have a swimming bath. The school's taking part in a new film to be called Thunder Birds and the film company will give enough to the sports fund to pay the cost of the pool. This movie, incidentally, is something of an international affair. The instructors in it are American, and some of the cadets are Chinese.

The food at the school is very good – plenty of fruit and salad, of course. And the British commanding officer had some urns put into the cafeteria, especially, so that the men should be able to get tea: for tea is one of the things America doesn't do quite so well as it does almost everything else.

One of the fine things about the life here is the way the people of the nearest town welcomed the cadets. They are really very good to them. The congregation of the Episcopal church holds a dance for them every week; and when a new course arrived, a few days before my visit, a mass invitation was sent to the school. Every single cadet was invited to the town, first to tea, and then to a dance, and finally to spend the night; and it isn't a very big place either. And not long ago, the Spanish Americans held a barbecue for them, of lambs; it's a special sort of feast, the barbecue; and that night everyone ate barbecued lamb. The school hasn't the means or facilities to return all this warm-hearted hospitality, but they do hold concerts in the cadets' lounge, which is a very pleasant room, and in the mess lounge. But the real point that strikes the visitor is that the cadets are part of the community.

This airport, which is so busy all the day, was almost desert six months ago. It's curious now to see the RAF at work among these foreign mountains; still more curious to wonder what the succession of young Britishers will mean to Arizona when the war is won; and what Arizona will mean to Great Britain, for it isn't the sort of place you could forget.

515 Squadron Personnel

The following are pilots and air gunners mentioned in the Operations Record Book (ORB) during 515's Moonshine and early Mandrel operations. (The author welcomes any further information on the aircrew listed):

Pilots	Fate (where known)
Squadron Leader Samuel Thomas	Later wing commander, DFC, AFC. Fought in the Battle of Britain with 264 Squadron. Appointed to command 3 Squadron but shot down in September 1943, ending the war as a POW.
Flight Lieutenant D.C. Wilkins	Posted out, 6.5.43.
Pilot Officer Stanley Hoskin	Promoted to A/F/L and appointed flight commander to take over from D.C. Wilkins (above).
Pilot Officer George Walters	Killed in action, 18.7.43.
Pilot Officer David Foster	Killed in action, 28.5.44.

Pilot Officer Arthur Sinton   Killed in action as a flying officer, 26.6.43.

Pilot Officer F. McGarry   Appointed acting flight lieutenant and flight commander, 15.2.43. Posted to 528 Squadron on 7.2.44 to undertake calibration flights.

Pilot Officer Bartholomew McKeon   Killed in action, 11.4.43.

Pilot Officer R. Schwarz

Warrant Officer Sydney Lewis

Warrant Officer Harry Whitmill   Killed in action, 10.4.44.

Flight Sergeant G.R. Armstrong

Flight Sergeant Frederick Steel   Killed in action, 8.6.43.

Flight Sergeant Thomas Macaulay   Killed in action, 21.5.43.

Flight Sergeant Robert Preston   Awarded the DFC in December 1944. Survived the war.

Flight Sergeant Lionel Anderson   Killed in action.

Flight Sergeant L.C. Woodward   Posted to 1 SLAIS Milfield (Special Low Attack Instruction School).

Sergeant S. Balam   Posted to 60 OTU on 26.2.44. Possibly S.H. Balam, RCAF – later a Tempest pilot with 501 Squadron.

Sergeant Thomas Ecclestone

Commissioned. Shot down and killed, 11.5.44.

Sergeant Ken Slade Betts

Shot down nineteen V1s and awarded the DFC. Killed in action on 29.12.44 flying Tempests with 3 Squadron.

Air gunners

Flight Lieutenant Derek Smythe

Posted to 307 TFU Bicester on 19.8.43. Gunnery leader with 223 Squadron in Celone, Italy. Awarded the DFC on 14.11.44. Survived the war.

Flying Officer Eric Ferguson

Killed in action, 11.4.43.

Pilot Officer R.G. Burgess

Pilot Officer Reg Dunbar

Posted to HQ 29 Group on 16.2.44. Retired from the RAF as a wing commander, DFM.

Pilot Officer Oswald Hardy

Posted to 21 OTU. Awarded the DFC on 23.3.45 as a flight lieutenant with 550 Squadron, Bomber Command.

Pilot Officer R. Shepherd

Posted to HQ 29 Group, 16.2.44.

Flight Sergeant Leonard Johnson

Commissioned on 7.5.43. Killed in action, 26.6.43.

Flight Sergeant G. Moon   Posted to 192 Squadron –
                                         a radio countermeasures
                                         (RCM) unit flying
                                         Wellingtons and Halifaxes.

Flight Sergeant Hugh Moule   Killed in action, 3.4.43.

Flight Sergeant T.R. Roberts   Posted to 10 AFU.

Flight Sergeant Albert Gray   Awarded the DFM.
                                         Commissioned. Killed in a
                                         flying accident on 8.6.43
                                         having previously survived a
                                         crash in October 1940.

Flight Sergeant George Neil   Killed in action, 18.7.43.

Flight Sergeant F. Ward

Flight Sergeant L.F. Green

Flight Sergeant J.E. Markey   Commissioned on 2.5.43.

Flight Sergeant R.B. Billows   Possibly Flight Sergeant Ralph
                                         Bernard Beresford Billows –
                                         an air gunner – who was
                                         killed in a flying accident with
                                         204 Squadron on 22.9.43.

Flight Sergeant Fred Gash   Commissioned in May 1943.
                                         Posted to HQ 25 Group on
                                         16.2.44. Survived the war.

Sergeant H. Jordan   Commissioned on 2.5.43.

Sergeant A.R. Flowerdew	Later warrant officer. Survived the war and served in the regular RAF, receiving a long-service award. He had served as a wireless op/air gunner with 8 Squadron in Aden in 1940 and completed thirty-one ops with 515 between November 1942 and the summer of 1943.
Sergeant W.A. Rowe	Posted to 11 OTU on 14.2.44.
Sergeant R. Newbon	
Sergeant Maurice Wilmer	Posted to 192 Squadron on 7.2.44. Killed in action on 25.4.44 as a flight sergeant, operating the specialist equipment.
Sergeant F. Tingle	Posted to 17 OTU. Possibly Frank Tingle – killed in action on 12.11.44 as a pilot officer.
Sergeant Geoffrey Wager	Killed in action, 21.5.43.
Sergeant S.R. Weston	Posted for pilot training.
Sergeant P.R. McLaren	Commissioned on 8.4.43.

515 Squadron Losses – 1943

3.4.43	Defiant AA542	Flight Sergeant Hugh Moule (air gunner) killed when parachute failed. Pilot safe.
11.4.43	Defiant AA417	Pilot Officer Bartholomew McKeon (pilot) and Flying Officer Eric Ferguson killed in action.
21.5.43	Defiant AA658	Flight Sergeant Thomas Macaulay (pilot) and Sergeant Geoffrey Wager killed in action.

8.6.43	Defiant AA435	Flight Sergeant Frederick Steel (pilot) and Pilot Officer Albert Gray killed in a flying accident.
25.6.43	Defiant AA572	Flying Officer Arthur Sinton (pilot) and Pilot Officer Leonard Johnson missing, presumed killed, in action.
18.7.43	Defiant AA651	Pilot Officer George Walters (pilot), an Australian, and Warrant Officer George Neil killed in action.

Sources

Official Documents

AIR27/1981	515 Squadron Operations Record Book.
AIR50/272	Combat report of Flight Lieutenant L.W.H. Welch.
AIR16/732	Assorted reports and maps on early Moonshine operations.
AIR16/733	Assorted documents regarding equipment deliveries, maintenance, modifications to aircraft, etc.
AIR2/7609	Minutes on particular raids.
AIR20/4743	Including notes relating to first Mandrel operations.
AIR20/1455	Further Mandrel operation reports, interim reports on effectiveness of jamming etc.

Publications

Aeroplane Monthly – April 1986.
Civil Defence in London, 1935–1945 – Robin Woolven (2001).
Willesden Chronicle – various copies, 1939–1945.

Further Reading

Bowman, Martin, *Confounding the Reich: The RAF's Secret War of Electronic Countermeasures in World War II* (Pen & Sword, 2004).

Chisholm, Roderick, *Cover of Darkness* (Chatto & Windus, 1953).

Clouston, A.E., *The Dangerous Skies* (Cassell, 1954).

Dawson, Jim, *The RAF in Arizona Falcon Field – 1941–1945* (Stenger-Scott, 2002).

Feast, Sean et al. *Bomber Command: Failed to Return II* (Fighting High, 2012).

Frankland, Noble and Webster, Sir Charles, *The Strategic Air Offensive Against Germany, 1939–1945*, Volume four, Annexes and Appendices (HMSO, 1961).

Shores, Christopher, *Those Other Eagles: A Tribute to the British, Commonwealth and Free European Fighter Pilots Who Claimed between Two and Four Victories in Aerial Combat, 1939–1982* (Grub Street, 2004).

Terraine, John, *The Right of the Line: The Royal Air Force in the European War, 1939–1945* (Hodder & Stoughton Ltd, 1985).

Personal Thanks

This book could not have been written without the support of a good many people. May I start by thanking Colin Higgs, a fellow enthusiast who introduced me to Lionel's nephew, Gerry's son, Jamie. From the first meeting with Jamie in a coffee shop in Henley, I knew that I wanted to write Lionel's story, and it has been a true privilege to have been entrusted with the task. Jamie's enthusiasm for the project has been constant, and he provided every support. This included putting me in touch with Stephen La Riviere, the 'go to' man for all things Gerry Anderson-inspired. Stephen's insight and our subsequent conversations and exchanges have proven invaluable, especially in piecing together Lionel's legacy and impact on his brother's creativity.

An enormous thanks goes to Wing Commander Reg Dunbar, DFM, RAF retd. Through a fabulous website (WONZ Forum) and a piece of good fortune by the name of Peter Wheeler, QSM, I was able to interview Reg about his time on 515 Squadron flying Moonshine and Mandrel sorties and learn so much more about the hazards they faced. I promised Reg and his son Richard that I would do all I could to tell the wider world about the achievements of that fine squadron in those dangerous days.

In terms of specifics, Larry A. Turner of the CAF Airforce Base in Arizona was most helpful in galvanising a team of willing helpers to provide insight into Falcon Field and identify Lionel's flying instructors, and steer me towards the most splendid book on the subject: *The RAF in Arizona Falcon Field – 1941–1945.* Nic Lewis of the 625 Squadron Association was also quick to respond to my hour of need, as was Dave Gibbs with his knowledge of Hunsdon; and my work colleagues Iona, Alex and Imogen – as ever – nodded in the right places and turned a blind eye to my occasional absences. Alex, I know, is ready to take commissions on research at The National Archives!

To my publisher in this venture, Steve Darlow, I am delighted to have collaborated on bringing Lionel's story to life. I have had the very good fortune of working with Steve on all of his 'Failed to Return' series and am thrilled to have taken our partnership to another level with this book.

In terms of my family, my mother has played a key role in keeping me on track against a very tight deadline by typing up all of Lionel's letters into an editable format. This saved me, quite literally, days if not weeks of work, and demonstrated that she's still quicker than anyone I know on the planet at typing real words. My brothers Stuart and Gary I would like to thank for their absolute and unquestioning love and support over more than forty years and for our shared love, admiration and respect for everything that Gerry Anderson created and the joy that it brought us as children, perhaps with the exception of the Mysterons.

And last, but not least, to my genius wife Elaine and teenage boys Matt and James – what can I say? I am now officially the shortest member of our family. Thanks guys.

Index